EMERGING TRENDS IN HIGHER EDUCATION

By Michael G. Strawser, James D. Breslin,
& Adam Elias

NEW FORUMS

NEW FORUMS PRESS INC.

Published in the United States of America
by New Forums Press, Inc. 1018 S. Lewis St.
Stillwater, OK 74074
www.newforums.com

Copyright © 2020 by New Forums Press, Inc.

All rights reserved. No part of this publication may be reproduced or transmitted in any form or by any means, electronic or mechanical, including photocopy, or any information storage or retrieval system, without permission in writing from the publisher.

Library of Congress Cataloging-in-Publication Data Pending

This book may be ordered in bulk quantities at discount from New Forums Press, Inc., P.O. Box 876, Stillwater, OK 74076 [Federal I.D. No. 73 1123239]. Printed in the United States of America.

ISBN 10: 1-58107-340-2
ISBN 13: 978-1-58107-340-9

Table of Contents

Introduction ix

Section I: Institutional Economics 1

Section I, Topic I — University Financial Overview 3
    The Best of Times 3
    The Worst of Times 5
        Public Perception 5
        Enrollment 5
        Affordability and Stability 6
        University "Business" 7
    Financial Landscape 8
    Financial Recovery 8
    Conclusion 9
    Ponder 10
    References 11

Section I, Topic II — Budgets and Business Models 13
    Budget Development 13
        What is a budget? 13
    Budget Principles 14
    Predictors 15
    Budget Models 16
        Incremental Budgeting 16
        Zero-Based Budgeting 16
        Activity-Based Budgeting 16
        Performance-Based Budgets 17
        Stakeholder Allocation 17
    Business Models 18
        Promises and Reorientation 18
        Discounting 19
        Operational Efficiencies 19
    Conclusion 19

Ponder	20
References	22
Section I, Topic III – Collaboration and Partnerships	23
Growing Partnerships	23
Career Development & Corporate Engagement	24
Community Engagement	24
Mergers	24
Credentials	24
Online Degree Partnerships	24
International Student Population	25
Additional External Partnerships	25
Internal Partnerships	26
Conclusion	26
Ponder	27
References	31
Section I, Topic IV – Alternate Revenue	33
A Philosophy of Revenue	34
Alternative Revenue in Higher Education	35
New Educational Revenue	35
Institutional Branding	36
Auxiliary Services and Campus Operations	36
Facilities and Real Estate	37
General Revenue	37
Traditional Revenue Generation	37
Cost-Savings	38
Institutional Culture	39
Conclusion	39
Ponder	40
References	41
Section I, Topic V – Brand: Distinction, Loyalty, and Marketing	43
Marketing	44
Influencer Marketing	44
Content Creation	44
Social Media Campaigns	45
Outlets	45

Admissions and Enrollment 46
    Campus Tours 46
    Admissions Requirements 46
    Enrollment 47
Recruitment 47
Technology and Recruitment Tools 47
Communication Tools 48
    Reality-Shaping Devices 48
    Retention 48
Conclusion 50
Ponder 50
References 51

Section II: Student Services 53
Section II, Topic I – Student Engagement Strategies 55
Foundations of Engagement 55
Engaging the 21st Century Student 56
    From Volunteerism to Social Responsibility 57
    Overreliance on Residential Programming 58
    Multidisciplinary and Faculty-Staff
        Partnerships Matter 59
Student Engagement in a Post-Obama, Post-Truth
    World 59
    Politics on Campus 60
    Food and Housing Insecurity 60
Ponder 61
References 62
Section II, Topic II – Space and Facilities 63
Student Utilization of Campus Spaces 64
Policies, Politics, and Legalities 65
Aligning Space Allocation and Institutional Values 67
Master Planning, Capital Projects, and Universal
    Design 68
    Capital Projects and Private-Sector Partnerships 69
    Universal Design as an Equity Issue 69
Ponder 70

References 72
Section II, Topic III – The Student Experience........................73
   Experiences in the Curricular Spectrum 73
      The Formal Curriculum 74
      The Co-Curriculum..76
   Institutional Services..77
   Framing Online Experiences as a Seamless Part of
      the Student Experience 78
   The Student Experience and Their Continual
      Evaluation of the Value Proposition.............................79
   Ponder 80
   References..81
Section II, Topic IV – Career Development.............................83
   That's Not My Job 83
   Careers, Gen Eds, and the Liberal Arts................................84
   Who Should Career Services Serve? 85
   Interconnectedness of Academic and Career Advising........86
   Career Advising as Central to the Work of Staff
      and Faculty..87
   Engaging Key Constituents...88
   Ponder 88
   References..90
Section II, Topic V – Advising and Student Guarantees..........91
   Contemporary Advising Practice..92
   Emerging Next Practices in Advising...................................93
   Pie Crust Promises: Student Guarantees..............................95
      On-time Graduation 95
      Study Abroad and Internships....................................96
      Guarantees as Marketing Tool 97
   Ponder 98
   References..99
Section II, Topic VI – Social and Political Engagement........101
   Uncomfortable Conversations and
      Controversial Speakers 102
   Safe Spaces and Trigger Warnings.....................................103
   Political Engagement For and By Who?............................105

Politicization of Education on Human Dignity
and Social Consumerism...106
Ponder 108
References...109

Section III: Teaching and Learning............................111
Section III, Topic I – Course Delivery...............................113
   The Internet as the Great Disrupter............................113
   Blended Delivery 116
   The Future of Education Delivery 118
   Ponder 119
   References..121
Section III, Topic II – Learning Environments 123
   Classrooms...123
   Community-Based Learning..124
   Learning Management Systems..................................127
   Ponder 130
   References..132
Section III, Topic III – Media Platforms............................133
   Modern Materials..134
   Benefits 135
   A New Frontier in eCommerce 137
   Open Education Resources 138
   Ponder 140
   References..142
Section III, Topic IV – Teaching at Scale 143
   The Severity of Scale...144
   Multimedia...145
      Web-Conferencing 147
      Adaptive Learning 149
      Caution...149
   Ponder 150
   References..152
Section III, Topic V – Pedagogical Strategies I:
   Deconstructing the Traditional....................................153
   Competency-Based Education 153

Open Learning 157
Ponder 159
References 161
Section III, Topic VI – Pedagogical Strategies II:
Gamification & Immersive Learning 163
Gamification 163
Immersive Learning 166
Ponder 168
References 170

About the Authors **173**

Introduction

As the higher education market becomes more saturated with competition and as enrollment demographics continue to shift, universities must become more adept at developing, implementing, and promoting strategic initiatives. Recently, Bellarmine University, a private liberal arts institution in Louisville, KY, created a new strategic plan. The strategic planning process was a campus-wide initiative bringing together faculty, staff, and administrators. This resource was inspired by that strategic planning process.

My colleagues and I played integral roles in the strategic planning process during our time at Bellarmine and, even though I am now a professor at the University of Central Florida, I initiated a project focused on helping other institutions plan strategically for their next phase. This resource mimics our time together working on the strategic plan. I am a faculty member, Dr. Breslin is Bellarmine's Assistant Provost for Assessment, Accreditation, and Institutional Effectiveness and former Dean of Student Success, and Adam Elias is Bellarmine's Director of Innovative Learning Systems.

Each author created a section that either connects directly to their expertise or is connected to their experiences during the strategic planning process. This resource is applicable for any institution and provides a structured, readable, and applicable strategic planning resource. As an overview of emerging trends, this book can be used by faculty, staff, and administrators alike to evaluate current institutional dynamics in light of national and international trends. The authors, like those in your own institutions, may not agree on every point, and you will see that play out across these pages, but differing perspectives provide value.

This resource includes questions to ponder at the end of every chapter that can help small groups and work groups think strategically about next steps. The book is divided into three easy to read sections: Institutional Economics (exploring university finances); Student Services; and Teaching and Learning.

We hope you enjoy.

                      Michael G. Strawser
                      Assistant Professor, Communication
                      University of Central Florida

Section I
Institutional Economics

By Michael G. Strawser

Institutional Economics
University Financial Overview

University faculty and staff may not be privy to institutional "numbers," and the siloed nature of some universities creates an environment where it is hard to see the grand financial forest through the trees, so to speak. While it is absolutely essential to have a clear understanding of your own institutional financial picture, it is also helpful to have a clear, or at least informed, perspective about the state of higher education in the United States, broadly. Unfortunately, many institutions are dealing with similar concerns and challenges that, sadly, may also limit innovative programs and instruction. While the situation is not apocalyptic, the current financial trends in the higher education market are worth considering. This section, then, will address market-positives and, of course, market-negatives, that generally impact higher education as a whole. To see a clear picture of the dilemma, we can turn to Charles Dickens (1867), who may have said it best:

> It was the best of times, it was the worst of times, it was the age of wisdom, it was the age of foolishness, it was the epoch of belief, it was the epoch of incredulity, it was the season of light, it was the season of darkness, it was the spring of hope, it was the winter of despair.

The Best of Times

Higher education professionals recognize the immense importance of a college degree. Typically, admissions officers will tout the lifetime earnings of degree holding students compared to those without (same with graduate degree earners compared to solely undergraduate completers). The fiscal impact of a college graduate may be sufficient enough, but the benefits of earning a college degree go beyond financial security and, with the ever-increasing number of student loans, the financial argument still exists, but is harder to sell. College graduates do earn more and enjoy more certainty when it comes to employment. In 2017, a Pew Research report even found that college degree holders have increased job satisfaction. The quality-of-life dynamic cannot be understated. With that said, college graduates also tend to volunteer more often in their communities, have a higher degree (or level) of "happiness," and degree attainment can lead to improved health and life-expectancy. Indeed, in this regard, life after a degree is the best of times.

There is additional good news. The National Center for Education Statistics reports:

> Between 2000 and 2016, educational attainment rates among 25- to 29-year-olds increased. During this time, the percentage who had received at least a high school diploma or its equivalent increased from 88 to 92 percent, the percentage with an associate's or higher degree increased from 38 to 46 percent, the percentage with a bachelor's or higher degree increased from 29 to 36 percent, and the percentage with a master's or higher degree increased from 5 to 9 percent. (para. 1)

Ultimately, this means more individuals are attaining an advanced degree. An increase in educational attainment is a distinguishing factor of "the best of times."

Quality of life and educational attainment represent two of the more prominent arguments for an encouraging outlook on higher education. Yet, even beyond direct impact on degree earners, higher education has seen a renaissance of student learning as new modalities and transformative instructional strategies have arisen out of a necessity to serve the modern student. Additionally, many campuses continue to diversify as more first generation and minority students are pursuing, and finishing, college degrees. Also, it could be argued that the sheer magnitude of the changing narrative of higher education may lead to a new dawn, so to speak.

All is not lost.

The Worst of Times

While there is nothing new under the sun, the true reality of the college landscape is dire or, at the very least, challenging. A number of factors directly influence the current financial challenges many institutions are facing.

Public Perception

Although higher education professionals, especially in recent decades, have become more aware of negative public perception of colleges and their degree offerings, the outcry has recently become more prominent. Take, for instance, a recent survey that revealed 55% of adults think colleges and universities have a positive impact on American society, while 36% believe there is a negative impact (Pew Research Center, 2017). Most Americans still believe a college degree is essential (Lederman, 2017), but the spike in mistrust and overall negativity surrounding colleges and universities is cause for concern. Public perception has also become more partisan as Pew (2017) also revealed that a majority of Republicans say colleges and universities are hurting the country because institutions are becoming too liberal (Auter, 2017). Does data reveal a college apocalypse? Absolutely not, but it is worth paying attention to increasingly volatile public perception of postsecondary education.

Enrollment

Enrollment trends are also staggering and reveal embedded long-term challenges for all institutions, public and private. The National Center for Education Statistics revealed that the number of high school students seeking a postsecondary degree has grown but the total overall number of high school students in some states has dipped (Hussar & Bailey, 2014). Ultimately, the "total net" is shrinking in some states despite the increase in degree conferrals. Demographic shifts, including a potential rise in Hispanic and Asian/Pacific Islander students and potential slips in African American and White students, may create a new admissions pool and student-focus areas. In the past 8 years, undergraduate enrollment at private institutions increased 38%; however, over the next 8 years there is a projected increase of only 10% (National Center for Education Statistics, 2018). College Board, in their Trends in Higher Education series, revealed:

> Between 2010 and 2015, enrollment rose by 5% (340,000 students) at public four-year colleges and universities and by 6% (203,000 students) in the private nonprofit sector. Enrollment fell by 11% (908,000 students) at public two-year colleges and by 33% (677,000 students) in the for-profit sector. (p. 4)

It should also be mentioned that while degree conferrals are increasing (see The Best of Times), degree completion (i.e. retention), continues to be problematic:

> Less than fifty percent of students complete their degree within six years. Although many of these students transfer and complete their education at another university, a large number never finish. This includes both two-year and four-year institutions. As many as one in three students drop out entirely and never finish their degrees. (Allaire, 2018, para 14).

We may continue to see stagnant growth at best, and lower retention rates which, obviously, influence all institutions but may have a greater impact on tuition-driven universities.

Affordability and Stability

As if the rise in negative public perception and potential for decreased enrollment were not enough, higher education professionals must also deal with increasing degree costs and job market disruptions. Unfortunately, since the 2008 recession the cost of tuition has increased 28 percent (Young Invincibles, 2016). College Board (2017) says that in 2017-2018

> ...the median tuition and fee price for full-time students attending private nonprofit four-year institutions is [was] $35,260. However, 10% of full-time students attend[ed] institutions with prices below $12,000 and 13% attend institutions charging $51,000 or more. (p. 3)

This constitutes a tuition hike compared to 2007-2008.

Between 2007-08 and 2017-18, published in-state tuition and fees at public four-year institutions increased at an average rate of 3.2% per year beyond inflation, compared with 4.0% between 1987-88 and 1997-98 and 4.4% between 1997-98 and 2007-08. (CollegeBoard, 2017, p. 3)

Ultimately, these numbers do not seem outrageous until you learn that the average student debt amount for an individual student is $30,000 (CollegeBoard, 2017).

Affordability is a concern, but career prospects have also been impacted because of economic disruptions and declining job security (Callanan, Perri, & Tomkowicz, 2017). What does this mean for us? College students are paying more for a degree and while degree completers typically earn more wages over time, job market instability and an increase in technical skill requirements for employees may influence degree seekers. In most states, income has remained stagnant while the cost of college has increased.

University "Business"

The University, itself, is changing. Students have become increasingly consumer-minded when it comes to higher education, institutional operating costs continue to increase, and the new professoriate—increased time constraints, research and advising expectations, volatile Ph.D. job market, part-time instructors, etc.—continues to influence morale and effectiveness of university instructors.

Adam Harris (2018), in an article previewing potentially negative credit ramifications of institutions, said

...students and parents seek decreases in the cost of attendance, while expecting better services and amenities; and as the disparity between student expectations and willingness to pay continues to grow, the analysts wrote, it will further strain mid-level institutions. (para. 4)

What does all of this mean? All told, while there is nothing new under the sun, it certainly seems as though there is a "financial perfect storm" brewing.

Financial Landscape

Negative public perception, stagnant or declining enrollment, issues with affordability, and the changing nature of "higher education" are all factors that have led us to a place of financial confusion, and in some instances, despair. A 2017 *Survey of College and University Presidents* , conducted by Inside Higher Education, revealed troubling news:

- Six in 10 presidents strongly agree or agree they are confident their institution is financially sustainable over the next five years. Slightly less, 52 percent, are confident about their institution's financial health over the next 10 years, more than felt that way in 2016.
- College presidents' greatest concerns about enrollment are having enough institutional aid to enroll as many low-income students as their college would like to have, enrolling students who are likely to retain and graduate on time, and enrolling their college's target number of undergraduates.

Faculty, staff, students and even university boards certainly feel financial constraints, but to realize that 40% of presidents are concerned about their institution's short-term (five year) financial viability and almost 50% are concerned about long-term (ten year) financial viability reveals yet another tangible obstacle.

Financial Recovery

The new financial landscape may lead to several different avenues for additional revenue or cost consolidation. Some of these options will be discussed, more in depth, in subsequent sections. As institutions face uncertain financial futures, decreasing enrollment and, in some cases, decreased state funding, new avenues must be explored. For instance, to combat total student debt that has surpassed one trillion dollars, Purdue University is developing a "pay-after" model where students will agree to pay the university a percentage of their post-graduation income. Some universities, through direct measures like mergers, or other more subtle programs, have enacted shared institutional service models. And, as has been and will always be the case, institutions may rely on instructors and staff to continually do more with less, as personnel may dwindle on certain campuses.

Conclusion

As institutions continue to identify emerging economic trends, it is important to remember that although the situation may seem insurmountable at times, higher education has experienced moments of financial distress in the past. We can easily review the last five decades as an example of negative campus narratives. Mintz (2017) astutely points out that the issues we are currently experiencing are, at the very least, regurgitated challenges in some form or fashion. In the "recent" past, the market was flooded with "books with such titles as *Higher Education in Crisis* (1995), *The Education Crisis* (1988), *Campus Unrest* (1970), *The Big Squeeze: Crisis on the Campus* (1946), and *Crisis on the Campus* (1900)" (Mintz, 2017, para. 27). Yet, this time may be different (Mintz, 2017). In some ways we face unprecedented financial challenges that threaten the structure of higher education, a structure that has survived without major change for centuries. Institutions must be prepared for this new landscape, a context that calls for massive institutional and organizational assessment. While finances are only part of the problem, an institution's budget, mounting student debt, and decreased funding, and stagnant enrollment numbers compound issues that are impacting every institution in some form or fashion.

Practically, faculty, staff, and even students should have a baseline understanding of how, and why, higher education, at least in the United States, is in its current situation. In many ways, still, this is the best of times. In 1870, a mere 50,000 people attended university and today those numbers have skyrocketed past 15/20 million. This increase in degree attainment is nothing short of remarkable. Pedagogy and instructional strategy have evolved, probably for good reason, and the quality-of-life impact of degree attainment cannot be overstated. Yet, we cannot ignore the challenges that arise in what may seem like the worst of times; institutions must continue to address current concerns with student-centered and market-friendly innovation.

Ponder

How has your institution capitalized during the "best of times" (i.e. have degree conferrals increased, have student job placements become more relevant, have you noticed an increase in alumni job satisfaction)?

_____
_____
_____
_____
_____
_____
_____

How is your institution dealing with the following:
- Public Perception
- Enrollment
- Affordability and Sustainability
- University "Business"

_____
_____
_____
_____
_____
_____
_____

Make a list of five big picture ideas that could help your institution move past the current financial crisis (assume that these ideas are "blank check"—do not allow money to impact your creativity at this time):

1)
2)
3)
4)
5)

References

Auter, Z. (2017, December 27). What Gallup learned about higher education in 2017. Retrieved from https://news.gallup.com/opinion/gallup/224444/gallup-learned-higher-education-2017.aspx

Callanan, G. A., Perri, D. F., & Tomkowicz, S. M. (2017). Career management in uncertain times: Challenges and opportunities. *The Career Development Quarterly*, *65* (4), 353-365.

CollegeBoard. (2017). Trends in college pricing 2017. Retrieved from CollegeBoard website: https://trends.collegeboard.org/sites/default/files/2017-trends-in-college-pricing_0.pdf

Dickens, C. (1867). *A tale of two cities, and great expectations* (Diamond ed.). Boston, MA: Ticknor and Fields.

Harris, A. (2018, January 23). Outlook for higher ed in 2018 is bleak, ratings agency says. Retrieved from https://www.chronicle.com/article/Outlook-for-Higher-Ed-in-2018/242319

Hussar, W. J., & Bailey, T. M. (2014). Projections of education statistics to 2022. *NCES 2014-051*, Washington, DC: National Center for Education Statistics.

Mintz, S. (2017). 11 lessons from the history of higher ed. Retrieved from https://www.insidehighered.com/blogs/higher-ed-gamma/11-lessons-history-higher-ed

National Center for Education Statistics. (2018). Fast facts enrollment. Retrieved from https://nces.ed.gov/fastfacts/display.asp?id=98

Pew Research Center. (2017). Sharp partisan divisions in views of national institutions. Retrieved from http://www.people-press.org/2017/07/10/sharp-partisan-divisions-in-views-of-national-institutions/

Young Invincibles. (2017). Higher education. *Young Invincibles*. Retrieved from http://younginvincibles.org/issues/higher-education/

Institutional Economics
Budgets and Business Models

Although no institution is immune to challenges of the current higher education market, some universities face more dire situations compared to others. While it is important to recognize where institutions may fall short in their fiscal projections, it is hard to grapple with financial truths if there is not an underlying foundation of financial knowledge. To help clarify baseline budgetary questions, this section will provide a general overview of institutional budgets and common business models and will provide a glossary of financial terms for which some administrators, faculty and students may lack familiarity and understanding.

Budget Development
What is a budget?

In our homes, a budget refers to our revenue versus expenditures. In any corporation, that umbrella understanding is similar. Ideally an institution would bring in more (revenue) than they spend (expenditures). Simple enough, right…? Well, clearly it is not that simple. Budgets at the higher education level can contain several different distinctions that are unique compared to our home budgets. For instance, at the institutional level we need to consider operating (keeping the lights on) expenses and debt as well as assets, state funding (if applicable) and endowment (a financial donation given for ongoing support)-among other budget categories. These categories can create confusion among faculty, staff and even students.

However, budgets are necessary! Budgets help institutions

steward their resources. Budgets can help forecast and plan for the future, they can control and allocate current resources, and budgets can help communicate organizational core values. Ultimately, budgeting can help your institution see, and move toward, the future. Budgets can also help institutions determine what money is unrestricted (like tuition) or restricted (like state funding) to make sure spending is ethical.

Budget Principles

For most institutions, budget discussions focus on revenue generated from students and expenditures used to pay for personnel (salaries and benefits) and day-to-day operations. Institutional budgets must consider financial aid, or discount rates for students, room and board revenue, and capital investments...and a host of other variables. In 2000, Deagelia M. Peña, in cooperation with the National Education Association, discovered eight variables related to most institutional budget models. These factors are helpful for thinking through and identifying budget categories and, while some variables may have become less (or more) prominent since the year 2000, the categories are still relevant. A modified, and simplified, table of Pena's factors is below (Table 1).

Table 1. Eight institutional budget model variables

Factor	Brief Description
Overall Financial Picture	The basic financial condition of the institution including revenues, expenditures, faculty and students.
Determinate Revenue and Expenditure	Consists of revenues and expenditures that are predetermined or earmarked for specific purposes (i.e. state and local appropriations or restricted revenue).
Revenues and Expenditures Ratio	Revenues and expenditures expressed as ratios to items such as full-time equivalency, etc.
Expenditures per full-time equivalency student	Full-time equivalency revenue is directly linked to expenditures.
Endowment	Unrestricted and total endowment income.

Building and equipment assets per full-time equivalency student	Building and equipment assets.
Government grants and contracts spent on public service and institutional support	The relationship between government grants and contracts and community service.
Other expenditures as ratios to education and general expenditures.	Library, maintenance, academic support, etc.

Most, if not all, income and expenses will fall into one of Peña's (2000) eight factors.

Predictors

A number of emerging factors will influence budgets and their projections moving forward. First, we know that enrollment will probably continue to remain flat or stagnant at most institutions. For institutions at which primary revenue is related to tuition, this could be problematic. Tuition continues to remain flat or stagnant for various reasons, but population changes and tuition costs continue to influence tuition revenue most vigorously. Remember, the National Center for Education Statistics (NCES) (2015) reported that in the past 8 years undergraduate enrollment at private colleges increased 38%, but the next 8 years the increase will be only 10%. High school graduation numbers may also decline, and the cost of college has grown while income has remained more stagnant and has not kept pace.

Second, the number of "traditional" college-age students is declining and there is greater competition for those remaining traditional students. Third, the rising student population is diversifying. Women, first generation college students, and Hispanic as well as Asian Pacific American numbers will increase. The instability of current student populations may be alarming, but ultimately this shows a market shift. In light of these shifting demographic numbers, how should institutions develop appropriate budget models?

Budget Models

The sections below highlight various budget models used in higher education. While the list is not exhaustive, this does serve as a template for a foundational or initial budget model exploration. While there are certainly models that are more popular or widespread, activity and performance-based budgets have become more common.

Incremental Budgeting

In their description of institutional budget models, Hanover Research (2013) identified an incremental budgeting model as the most traditional model we have today. In an incremental budget model, the budget is based on the revenue and expenditures of the previous year and, as such, moderate increases and cuts are made based on historical precedent. Incremental budgets are stable and allow for multi-year planning and are typically adjusted based on percentage. An incremental budget can be easy to administer and develop and does not emphasize future plans/initiatives.

Zero-Based Budgeting

This type of budget basically starts over every year. There is no real precedent or historical understanding. A zero-based budget will distribute resources based on need.

Activity-Based Budgeting

Hanover positioned Activity-Based Budgeting as an alternative to the traditional model. An activity-based budget will reward (by increased funding) those campus activities that see the greatest return. Think of this as a return-on-investment model. Instead of broad, or general expenses, like a department or school budget, an activity-based budget model will look at specific activities and budget accordingly.

Performance-Based Budgets

Performance-based budget models are similar to activity-based budgeting solutions, but the key factor is not solely revenue and instead is tied to several different performance-based outcomes. In an academic setting, this could be successful mission-related initiatives that aren't necessarily revenue-generating.

Stakeholder Allocation

Part of the challenge with emphasizing or even discussing various budget strategies is the difference between institutional goals and revenue allocation. In a centralized budget model, a university will typically collect resources/revenue into a "pot" and high-ranking administrators are primarily responsible for budget allocation. This is, at times, created in collaboration with a decentralized budget model that emphasizes unit or department autonomy and spending. A centralized budget enables key administrators to make hard decisions but can, at times, provide low motivation for individual units or departments to build revenue. On the other hand, a decentralized budget will emphasize departmental control and revenue. Tuition revenue for instance, will be collected and distributed within the academic department. In a decentralized budget model, revenue streams, fundraising, and, often, competition, are emphasized. A decentralized budget may also be referred to as a responsibility-centered model.

For reference, a summative budget model table is below in Table 2.

Table 2. Budget model descriptions

Budget Model	Description
Incremental	Based on the revenue and expenditures of the previous year and, as such, moderate increases and cuts are made based on historical precedent.
Zero-Based	The budget starts over every year. A zero-based budget will distribute resources based on need.
Activity-Based	Rewards (by increased funding) those campus activities that see the greatest monetary reward.

Performance-Based	Similar to activity-based budgeting but the key factor is not only revenue and instead is tied to several different performance-based outcomes.
Stakeholder Allocation	A decentralized budget will emphasize departmental control and revenue.

Again, the list of budget models above is not exhaustive, but a broad-strokes understanding should serve you well no matter your role. It may be time to revisit your institutional budget model or categorize differently based on the current enrollment and demographic projects.

Business Models

It is true that most institutions of higher learning are de-facto non-profit agencies. Yet, there will always be an onus on universities and colleges to sustain a revenue that can move the institution forward in the midst of rising costs and stagnant tuition numbers. The current financial landscape has provided an opportunity for institutions to change their business model to adapt to the times. While there is no shortage of ways to achieve this, a few possibilities stand above the rest.

Promises and Reorientation

While the discount rate remains high for many institutions (on average tuition can be discounted between 40-45% per student), universities recognize that this model may not be sustainable. To combat high discount rates for students, some universities have established four-year graduation guarantees or condensed bachelor's degree options to three years rather than the traditional four. Additionally, the advanced placement high school credit transfers have remained well-used, for some institutions, while competency-based education, even in the form of nanodegree or micro credentialing as seen in Massive Online Open Course offerings, has become even more prominent. Students with experience in a given area can design a portfolio to showcase specific skills and transfer those "credits" to some accredited institutions.

Discounting

Discounting has become a more popular avenue to make tuition-driven institutions, especially, more competitive. Institutions may offer a substantial discount rate, meaning, the actual "cost-to-attend" is dramatically different compared to the sticker cost that is published on marketing materials. To address the discount rate, the federal government mandated that a net cost calculator be implemented on college websites. Institutions that "discount" may guarantee a price point that would eliminate the threat of a tuition reduction or offer substantial financial aid and scholarship opportunities.

Operational Efficiencies

While it is true that enrollment numbers may vary, the cost of enhancing the college student experience continue to rise. As such, as a more efficient business model, some institutions are eliminating or streamlining operational waste and, as a result, classes may be spread out through different times/days on brick-and-mortar campuses, hybrid (or online/onsite blended courses) may be more popular, or institutions may offer purely online course offerings. Some institutions, to increase operational efficiency, have also significantly cut "administrative bloat."

Conclusion

Institutions without a clear and sustainable budget will continue to suffer in the years to come. It is important, especially for those institutions with little to no history of budget transparency, to create open lines of communication in these trying times. Colleges and universities may have to consider a variety of factors in the midst of this institutional transformation.

There should be some semblance of shared budgetary responsibility in higher education. This means faculty, staff and administration, and even students to a certain extent, should have a role in budgetary considerations in some capacity. This may not call for full-blown transparency, but stakeholders across campus can be utilized as innovative catalysts to consider budget decisions. Without a proper fundamental understanding of postsecondary budgets—influencing factors, categories, and budgeting models—transformative change may fall short.

Ponder

Who is the budget "decision-maker" at your institution?

___

If you had a budget recommendation, what is the process for approval?

___

What are your shared governance models to ensure budget transparency and implementation?

___

What may (or does) complicate budget initiatives at your institution?

In what ways does your institution's strategic plan influence "you" (and either your unit/department's spending, revenue, etc.)?

References

Hanover Research. (2013). 6 alternative budget models for colleges and universities [Blog post]. Retrieved from https://www.hanoverresearch.com/insights-blog/6-alternative-budget-models-for-colleges-and-universities/.

Pena, D. M. (2000). Higher education finance variables: An analysis. *The NEA 2000 Almanac of Higher Education*, 91-100.

Institutional Economics
Collaboration and Partnerships

As the landscape changes, institutional partnerships become even more appealing (and important). Universities must innovate and part of that innovative mentality can include collaboration and partnerships. Partnerships, especially external, allow institutions to think creatively and respond to current student and marketplace needs. As an emerging trend, collaboration allows institutions to provide creative opportunities for students no matter the level and availability of resources. While there are more types of partnerships, generally, than the examples listed below, the samples in this section provide a framework for how, and why, post-secondary institutions would partner with external stakeholders. Thus, this section will explore the emerging trend of partnerships from both external and internal perspectives.

Growing Partnerships

The economic realities of the United States have, yet again, revealed a deep-rooted higher ed debate—the importance and necessity of professional or career skills training. In many ways, the workforce is calling for workplace readiness and pragmatic skills, and institutions typically are tasked with finding new and innovative approaches that answer the challenge. External partnerships can help establish career connections for institutions, but they can also accomplish much more.

Career Development & Corporate Engagement

External partnerships, for most institutions, are driven and navigated by a rise in career development center importance (more on this below) and the need for universities to reiterate the value of a college degree. Some institutions begin career exploration immediately upon a student's admission, using enhanced assessments and pinpointed curricula to heighten career readiness.

Even liberal arts institutions are breaking down institutional silos and developing deeper relationships. Some institutions are partnering directly with corporations, like Amazon Web Services Academy or are allowing institutional and community networks to drive student placement. The move to outsource or develop connections beyond university walls has has again shifted the market.

Tuition-based programs, like Starbucks' partnership with Arizona State, illustrate a ripe avenue for collaborative and innovative thinking. Or, consider the recent move by the restaurant group that owns Chili's and Maggiano's to partner with Pearson Education to provide cost-free educational programs for employees. McDonald's also offers employees the opportunity to participate in their Archways to Opportunity program where employees can complete college course credit. Disney has also started a higher education program to cover tuition costs for hourly employees. Mostly these initiatives look similar to tuition remission of the past but the increasing call for corporations to partner directly with a university (i.e. Starbucks and Arizona State) has become more commonplace. Corporations have been partnering with institutions for generations but the trend has become more established and more structured.

One emerging theme, gathering steam in institutions across the world, is the rise of the career development center. As students and parents continue to question if college is a fiscally responsible choice, campus career centers have experienced a renaissance. Career services staff once focused solely on résumé and interview skills, but now employees in those positions find themselves in need of the skill set of a visionary, externally focused leader who can engage and connect with stakeholders. In many ways the career center can be the campus hub for external partnerships. Career center employees are responsible for navigating community-partnerships, delivering analytic data regarding job placement, all while counseling students on the in's and out's of the job search process. Ultimately, career centers can be campus catalysts for corporate engagement. The explosion of career services has also led to an increase in alumni networks or mentorship programs.

Community Engagement

Community engagement has also become a renewed focus for the academy. At Bellarmine University, for instance, the recent QEP (quality enhancement plan for SACS-COC accreditation) centered on inclusivity and community engagement. The community-engagement angle is not unique to 21st century higher education and, in fact, has been part and parcel to postsecondary education for centuries. Even before the co-creation of community solutions that we see now, institutions would function as a means to help establish and clarify democratic ideals (Fitzgerald et al., 2012). Many have advocated for an internal or global civic engagement for institutions focused on issues like alleviating poverty, improving public health, achieving universal primary and secondary education, and enabling locally controlled economic development (Watson et al., 2011; Laing, 2016). Because of the history and continued relevance of civic engagement in the academy, it should not surprise us that institutions continue to navigate communal waters.

Practically, community partnerships can be achieved in various ways. Service-learning has become even more of a focal point as younger generations want to explore volunteerism and engage in experiential learning. Additionally, service opportunities, clinical sites, collaborative community-institution programs, etc. are growing in sustained popularity.

Mergers

Because of financial realities, mergers have become a topic of conversation more so than they were in the past. Seltzer (2017) believes "Mounting fiscal pressures on higher education institutions would seem to have created a ripe environment for mergers between colleges and universities" (para. 1). Yet, he goes on to mention how some university administrators remain unconvinced of the validity of mergers, mostly because of the difficulty of implementation. Despite this difficulty, mergers have become more commonplace. TIAA recently released a report on the potential benefits of mergers, however difficult they may be. The report established that, yes, mergers can be challenging to implement, though can result in both financial savings and re-energized stakeholders (Azziz, Hentschke, Jacobs, Jacobs, & Ladd, 2017). Not all mergers result in fewer institutions; a synthetic merger is a kind of joining that results in shared services, while each institution retains its individual identity.

Credentials

While this is not a direct form of partnership, it will be interesting to see how traditional higher education institutions navigate micro-credentials (i.e. earning a micro-credential or mini-degrees or certifications in a specific topic area) and nanodegrees (i.e. a project and skills-based educational credential program) offered by online companies like Udacity, Udemy, and Coursera. Recently, the American Council on Education began testing and discussing offering credit for low-cost and free course offerings from online providers. Education credentialing has become a trend that, in some ways, has bypassed the traditional university.

Online Degree Partnerships

Credentials and nanodegrees will continue to increase, but traditional universities will also find ways of expanding connections with online providers. The University of Pennsylvania now offers a full online degree in computer and information technology. While other institutions have instituted a similar model, this is Coursera's first Ivy League Degree option. Coursera reaches over 30 million users and their collaborative degree programs with traditional "brick-and-mortar" institutions could be a trending collaborative opportunity for many institutions.

International Student Population

Traditionally, the U.S. has established a strong presence in the global academic community by attracting international students. Recently, however, the total number of international students on M (for vocational and nonacademic courses of studies) or F (for students who will be attending and academic program or full-time degree program at a university, school, or college which is approved by U.S. Immigration and Customs Enforcement) visas has declined-albeit slightly. Both policy reform and an increasingly competitive international market may complicate international relations as US institutions attempt to recruit and enroll international students.

Additional External Partnerships

While corporate partnerships, community engagement and institutional mergers are important, they are not the only opportunities for external partnerships. Universities can consider collaborative relationships with external research organizations, partnerships with government agencies or other publicly-funded mechanisms, or partnerships with universities that enable sharing of resources or expertise (i.e. joint-degree program offerings, consortium-type course selections). In California, Samuel Merritt University and Holy Names University signed an agreement to explore the potential of sharing one single property. These partnerships enable universities with limited resources to provide high-quality course offerings or experiences to their students.

Provider partnerships have also become more ingrained in university culture. For instance, some institutions may contract out what were once internal tasks including: course design and delivery for online offerings; marketing and recruitment; food service; information systems management or even human resources initiatives. Institutions considering external providers that constitute a service-based provision should consider how the partnership fulfills a strategic initiative and how the partnership achieves what could not have been accomplished in-house.

Internal Partnerships

External university partnerships are obviously important for growth and sustainability. But, an increase in internal partnerships seems to be a normalizing, and in some case stabilizing, factor for many institutions. CUNY, for instance, has a deeply-rooted initiative to increase diversity, equity and inclusion efforts that transcends either academic or student affairs. Purdue University, in an effort to meet current student needs and answer market demand, created a "data science for all" ecosystem that will make data science education part of every student's learning experience on campus. Recently, the University of Kentucky implemented a "Communication across the curriculum" initiative to drive campus-wide training and engagement related to multimodal (oral, written, digital) communication. Some institutions also offer dual-degree, especially for students pursuing a J.D., as students would complete a law-degree and second graduate degree simultaneously. Students can also complete accelerated degree programs which allow for the completion of a bachelor's degree and a graduate degree in less time than it would take to get each degree separately. Accelerated programs give both undergraduate and graduate credit for some courses, resulting in faster progress through the curriculum and, in some cases, these programs can be cross-disciplinary, meaning a student could complete their undergraduate degree in one field and still get an accelerated master's degree in a different subject-matter.

Conclusion

The partnerships mentioned above have, obviously, resulted in varying success depending on initiative resources and overall strategic implementation. Ultimately, as an emerging trend, it is important to remember that university partnerships, generally, are not new nor are they novel. However, partnerships are normalizing and becoming more common at both public and private institutions. The real trend is the popularity of the partnerships mentioned above and the realization that institutions no longer have the "siloed" option. It is imperative today that institutions develop external and internal partnerships that foster a spirit of collaboration.

If approached strategically (this is the key), the benefits of establishing campus partnerships may outweigh the challenges associated with developing new programming or creating new relationships. Partnerships will never be seamless, as each party will have its own end goal(s) and vision for the collaboration, but the chance to invigorate student professional experience, engage the community, save on operational costs, etc. cannot be ignored.

Ponder

How can your institution foster a culture of innovation as it relates to developing and sustaining partnerships?

_____
_____
_____
_____
_____
_____
_____

What beneficial partnerships has your institution enacted?

_____
_____
_____
_____
_____
_____

How can your institution be more collaborative with external partners?

_____
_____
_____
_____
_____
_____
_____

How may credentials change the value of a traditional college degree program?

_____
_____
_____
_____
_____
_____
_____
_____

Would your institution benefit from a true or synthetic merger? If yes, how? If no, why not?

_____
_____
_____
_____
_____
_____
_____
_____

References

Fitzgerald, H. E., Bruns, K., Sonka, S. T., Furco, A., & Swanson, L. (2012). The centrality of engagement in higher education. *Journal of Higher Education Outreach and Engagement, 16*(3), 7-27.

Laing, S. (2016). Community engagement is what universities should be for. Retrieved from https://www.timeshighereducation.com/blog/community-engagement-what-universities-should-be

Seltzer, R. (2017). The merger vortex. Retrieved from https://www.insidehighered.com/news/2017/08/01/higher-ed-mergers-are-difficult-likely-grow-popularity-speakers-say

Watson, D., Hollister, R., Stroud, S. E., & Babcock, E. (2011). *The Engaged University: International Perspectives on Civic Engagement.* London: Routledge.

Institutional Economics
Alternate Revenue

As universities worldwide deal with smaller endowments, shrinking tuition dollars (and enrollment), as well as frozen budgets, the question of alternative revenue source(s) becomes even more pressing. The previous model for most institutions, a framework that highlighted tuition and/or state funding, may need diversification in today's 21st century market. As state budgets tighten, and college competition becomes more fierce, universities would be wise to establish a portfolio of funds that moves beyond the traditional structure of today's model. With that said, developing a sustainable budget model that encourages alternate revenue is a difficult proposition.

State funding continues to be a source of concern. Public universities desire more control over enrollment, tuition, and developing programs and initiatives that compete in today's higher education marketplace. The goals of state legislators, who appropriate university funding, may not be the same. As a result, the discussion of state funding, for both public and private colleges (that rely on state funds for financial aid or research support) will continue to be a growing theme and concern. This may lead to an increase in privatized higher education. Practically, what does a privatized higher education system mean? Greater competition at the private ranks and a potential boon to alternative revenue streams. There are other factors to consider, however.

Administrators at institutions with lower endowment and minimal brand recognition have to get creative with how they balance budgets and contribute to a healthy bottom-line. The importance of such endeavors intensifies when you consider that creating alternate revenue streams will help protect students from bearing the burden of budgets in the red. Unfortunately, some institutions may be unwilling, or more likely unable, to establish a revenue stream that goes beyond the traditional teaching, research, service model.

A Philosophy of Revenue

Despite increased tuition and student fees, operational college costs continue to rise for all institutions, not just those losing state appropriations. Ultimately, it is no longer feasible for institutions to rely on students to fit the bill for total expenditures. As a result, administrators and university boards must engage the market creatively. While some may bristle at the concept of education as a business (multi-billion dollar business in many circumstances), the reality of expenditures like building maintenance, increased salaries, and a heightened student experience rely on funds that may not be adequately provided for through traditional means. Colleges may desire increased revenue for various reasons, but primarily from a student perspective, increased revenue from sources beyond tuition can help keep college affordable. Not surprisingly, some faculty and staff members are resistant to a more corporatized model of post-secondary education (Castillo, 2017). Yet, current budget shortcomings and looming decreases in student population do not provide a positive outlook.

Practically, institutions may struggle to create an entrepreneurial culture on-campus that emphasizes revenue generating ideas. As you read the ideas below, consider: is your leadership capable of, or empowered to, establish additional streams of revenue; is there a potential culture-clash in the waiting between academics on-campus and those who may appreciate a more commercialized institution (the latter may not necessarily be the board of trustees); does your institution have an infrastructure set up to market their services, used broadly, to different organizations or stakeholders-other than students?

Interestingly enough, academics, not just administrators, are experiencing pressure to build and sustain revenue-generating ideas. Revenue, in this case, goes beyond the traditional federal grant application. At many institutions scholars are expected to have a public presence and build partnerships with corporations. Traditionally, especially at research-driven institutions, faculty members were expected to earn their keep through grant funding. This is still expected, however, with increasing grant competition, and sometimes fewer funding opportunities, the demand for academics to go beyond traditional models has increased.

Alternate Revenue in Higher Education

The Education Advisory Board released a thorough list of various revenue generating ideas that can be utilized by most, if not all, institutions. In their report, published in 2013, the EAB highlights seven different categories for revenue expansion: New Educational Revenues; Academic Entrepreneurship Infrastructure; Branding, Licensing and Affinity; Auxiliary Services; Student Fees; Campus Operations; and Facilities and Real Estate. The following sections draw heavily from EAB's ideas and concepts.

New Educational Revenue

New education revenues center on increasing enrollment specifically through instructional strategy or instruction-based initiatives. Internal student recruitment, for example, can be an effective strategy to retain current student populations through initiatives like early-entry graduate degree completion, summer learning and course offerings, online dual-enrollment, etc. Alternative educational revenue can also be fostered through greater offerings for master's degree programs (i.e. weekend or evening programs, interdisciplinary and flexible degree programs, or liberal studies degree programs). Education revenues can also be external, driven from within but reaching those outside of the institution. Corporate training, faculty consulting, and certification offerings are all examples of external education revenue streams. Faculty consulting services, that partnership with the institution, can settle on an agreed upon rate that satisfies the university and the faculty member. Additionally, some departments may be inclined to perform research tasks for local organizations or corporations for a fee.

Institutional Branding

While some institutions may be more marketable or recognizable, colleges and universities should be ready to capitalize when a branding opportunity comes their way. Recently, Loyola University Chicago experienced a phenomenal run in the NCAA basketball tournament. Their team continued to impress and one specific institutional stalwart, Sister Jean, became a marketer's dream. The Loyola University Chicago Ramblers experienced a merchandise sales boon just as they were in the midst of a capital campaign to raise 80 million, by 2020, to financially support students from disadvantaged families. Ultimately, in this case, merchandise sales skyrocketed as the institution took advantage of a primed situation.

Branding, however, goes beyond merchandise sales. Institutions looking for additional revenue can establish university license plates, branded novelty items (i.e., wine or spirits), and can build additional revenue through affinity partnerships with banks and lending firms. If your institution is so inclined, you can create partnerships for orientation activities, career fairs, or even specific academic departments.

Auxiliary Services and Campus Operations

Both auxiliary services and campus operations can impact the fiscal bottom line. Some institutions have developed campus-wide service opportunities for patrons and students including, but not limited to, express fine dining, laundry services, DVD rental kiosks, and favorable vendor relationships. Additionally, some universities see their operational dynamics as a favorable revenue platform. Campus operations can positively contribute to an institution's budget by selling administrative services (IT hosting, research centers, child care operations) or even creating an environment of sustainable energy and purchase agreements (solar panels, wind farm contracts, etc.). Campus operations, usually a drain on university resources, can be a financial boon if approached with creativity.

Facilities and Real Estate

Some campuses take a traditional route to improving revenue, such as increasing student fees. Others, though, approach their own facilities as revenue-enhancing avenues. Several institutions already rent out campus space for community or personal events, like conferences or weddings, and some even use their space to host farmers markets or develop an on-campus hotel. Long-term leasing and developmental joint ventures (like partnering with a developer on a research facility or faculty-housing) are also not unheard of. Finally, a growing trend includes asset acquisition, or disposal, depending on the current needs of the institution. Universities may have real estate gifted to them by a donor or may even purchase real estate that will build future revenue.

General Revenue

Institutions can generate revenue in endless ways beyond the traditional. Universities can consider custom publishing and print shops as part of their portfolio. Creating a university-owned domain and selling advertising on a university website may also contribute additional funds. While many institutions may feel uncomfortable with such an enterprise, licensing courses or continuing education programs, like Boston University, can establish a consistent means of building revenue.

Traditional Revenue Generation

The ideas listed above are less traditional, focusing on new initiatives or a more corporate implementation. Meaning, they focus primarily on new initiatives or a more corporate implementation. Yet, some revenue generation strategies can be accomplished without a holistic spending spree or the development of new concepts or ideas. For one, universities can continue to focus on their own (current) student populations by increasing retention efforts. Retaining students can be a financial boon to institutions and the difference between a budget in the black and a budget shortfall. Second, universities may consider increasing enrollment efforts of non-traditional students. This can be accomplished by designating new recruitment strategies or by making student transfers easier and more student-friendly. A comprehensive strategic approach to pursuing non-traditional students may involve considering new modalities, such as flexible online and hybrid degree programs Third, industry and corporate partnerships enable universities to either provide revenue regeneration alongside student experience or enjoy an intentional means of bringing local and regional partners to campus to use campus resources. Finally, fundraising efforts and philanthropic engagement is always a safe means of securing additional revenue-as long as donors are willing, active, and able to give. In this vein, universities can make a concerted effort to reach new alums and build a donor base of recent graduates (the last 3-5 years). Some institutions have created staff positions or departments specifically to engage recent alumni.

Cost-Savings

All of an institution's financial woes may not need to be addressed by generating new revenue. Instead, universities may consider enacting cost-saving mechanisms to balance their budget. Limiting operational budgets, by closing or more efficiently using campus space, can save millions over time. Even something as simple as temperature and room lighting controls can help defray institutional costs. Environmentally friendly initiatives, like solar panels or water saving devices, can establish a campus environment-ethos but will also save colleges operating costs. Finally, it may also behoove institutions to maximize efficiencies across academic programs within academic programs or departments. To do this, consider your course catalog and identify course learning outcome overlap. Then, offer one cross-listed course that can satisfy the learning outcomes of both classes.

Institutional Culture

While the ideas above may sound exciting, or at the very least tolerable, institutions should remember that developing alternative revenue on-campus is not for the faint of heart. Typically, several of the ideas listed above will require university expenditure before revenue increases. Universities should ask whether the risk justifies the reward. And, as such, what are the costs of implementing such a cultural shift? Will administrators, faculty or staff be resistant? Or, has your institution developed the infrastructure to enact various ideas without negatively affecting student learning? These are just a few questions to consider when implementing new revenue streams.

Conclusion

The fiscal reality of most institutions has changed dramaticallty over the past few years. Institutions would do well to, at the very least, consider cost-saving initiatives to balance a budget. Those colleges and universities that are a little more risk-tolerant may do well to establish a financial inroad that transcends their current, and somewhat traditional, budget model. Alternative revenue streams should not be a decision of one particular individual, as most ideas will impact the broader campus community. Instead, the movement toward revenue-generation (beyond tuition dollars or endowment) can be a collaborative campus discussion. Your institution should consider the emerging trend of alternative revenue streams. The ideas presented above represent a slim margin of potential considerations. Hopefully, though, they can serve as a preliminary discussion starter that allows for the consideration of strategies related to broader campus infrastructure, mission and vision. The movement toward alternative revenue should not be approached lightly and instead should be considered in light of broader institutional goals.

Ponder

How is your institution already exploring alternative revenue streams?

_____
_____
_____
_____

Brainstorm (list) some dream-scenario (not necessarily feasible) alternative revenue ideas that your institution could enact and implement.

Brainstorm (list) some feasible alternative revenue ideas that your institution could enact and implement.

What revenue considerations does your institution need to think about (reduced state funding, declining enrollment, increased discount rate, etc.)?

Will alternative revenue streams help alleviate the considerations in number four or will they provide a sense of insurance? How?

References

Castillo, T. M. (2017, January 1). Traditional faculty resistance to the corporatization model in continuing education: A case study. *ProQuest LLC*.

Workman, J. (2014, January 6). Alternative revenues in higher education. Retrieved from https://www.eab.com/research-and-insights/business-affairs-forum/resources/alternative-revenues-in-higher-education

Institutional Economics

Brand: Distinction, Loyalty and Marketing

It is easy to assume that higher education has sold out—that we have become obsessed with branding and marketing our institutions and platforms. And, while branding and marketing have become more digitized and specialized, the purpose of this promotion isn't always to support learning. Further, although we would like to think generations past were purer and less relenting in this regard, David Grossman (2013) reiterates that marketing for enrollment purposes has always been a prominent practice in higher ed. Harvard and Columbia, at one point, were concerned about losing affluent students to other Ivy league institutions, so they revised admissions criteria and, even 100 years ago, institutions created the illusion of exclusivity to bolster enrollment (Grossman, 2013). As we consider marketing, broadly, we recognize that there is nothing new under the sun. Yet, the day is different and overwhelming market competition and unique student populations present dynamics ripe for new considerations for marketing and branding institutions.

The topics here reiterate emerging trends related to, generally, institutional promotion. While the categories and underlying cases are not exhaustive, they do provide a framework for understanding how marketing and branding have impacted retention, enrollment, admissions, and recruitment.

Marketing

As an emerging trend, marketing for higher education institutions has changed dramatically—especially the last five to ten years.

Influencer Marketing

Influencer marketing has become a popular outlet for a number of brands. Marketing for universities does not have to be celebrity-based. The use of influencers, or key leaders, to drive awareness on social platforms has become a routine practice. Yet, colleges can rely on social influencers who may not have celebrity status. Influential students, with substantial follower numbers, may be asked to contribute to the marketing strategy of the institution. However, students may also publish posts on their own accord that share experiences related to their college experience. In some cases, posts may go viral or may, at the very least, increase institutional awareness and web traffic. In essence, the university garners free brand awareness. Additionally, in this same vein, institutions can rely more heavily on reviews and online "word-of-mouth".

Content Creation

Generation Z (otherwise known as iGen, etc.), those born after 1996, have established YouTube as a preferred social platform. While video content does not monopolize university content creation, the development of videos, including student narratives, university tours, etc., has become a more pronounced university strategy. Video makes sense for various reasons, but the connection to the content consumption of iGen is a solid marketing strategy. Videos, when done well, can enhance the emotional appeal of an institution and when universities use appropriate storytelling techniques, videos can bring audiences into the institution's ethos. In fact, video advertisement effectiveness outweighs written or text-based advertisements. However, universities may also develop podcasts, magazines (available online and in print), and other media that could revolutionize awareness.

Social Media Campaigns

Social media marketing can take on numerous forms because of the sheer number of platforms and possibilities (e.g., Facebook banner ads, etc.). The benefits of social media are obvious. According to Smith and Anderson (2018), Facebook remains the primary platform for Americans, however, with younger generations, Instagram, Snapchat and YouTube remain popular social outlets. The sheer numbers, and potential for exposure, are substantial and institutions recognize that social integration can lead to increased interactions, an engaged current (and prospective) student community, and brand recognition. Social marketing campaigns tend to emphasize visual appeal and a consistent use of certain hashtags (#) to establish relevance and consistency. Ultimately, the user's specific experience must be in the forefront of university marketers With that said, similar to other marketing techniques, content can be created across platforms or for specific social tools. Additionally, many successful social media campaigns tend to create a community of users and rely heavily on current or former students (alums) to spread the message. Interestingly, it is not enough today for a university to have one singular social account (much less one specific platform). Instead, all facets of the institution tend to be marketed on social media—e.g., athletics, student life, etc.—often with their own accounts, managed by a variety of individuals, perhaps outside of a marketing/communications functional area. Social campaigns allow for user-generated statistics, number of clicks and other analytic-measures, to inform the strategy.

Outlets

Traditionally, paper-heavy campaigns sent through the postal service ruled the day. These days are not archaic, but the strategy has certainly become more intentional. It is not enough to simply assume your audience will respond to a brochure sent through the mail. Instead, marketing efforts have become concentrated on individual/unique users, and these same efforts have been developed for other avenues (e.g., mobile platforms). Media-rich design that targets potential audience members through ads and other strategic efforts have become more pressing and indeed more available. The increase in mobile availability, and tech-saturation even beyond mobile platforms, has allowed institutions to live stream and engage potential students through real-time events and accessibility. The impact of mobile has also changed institutional websites as many sites are now mobile friendly. This has impacted search rankings and has placed additional importance on website Search Engine Optimization.

Admissions and Enrollment

As one would expect, the marketing shift has also changed admissions and admission expectations. The prototypical strategic enrollment plan now has to compensate for a declining prospective student population and increased competition. As a result, admissions, broadly, has become more strategic at most institutions. Universities and colleges may now rely heavily on analytics to inform marketing procedures and on-campus visits.

Campus Tours

Campus tours, the stalwart and seminal admissions moment, have become increasingly more digital. Today, campuses can (and do) utilize Virtual Reality efforts to extend students a "feel-like-you-are-there" experience. Virtual tours allow students and parents to visit campus even if they cannot travel to the physical location. Additionally, the entire admissions process has moved, in most cases, to a digital format. Students can engage with their prospective campuses via virtual and augmented reality, but they also can engage on digital devices to get a feel for their campus fit.

Admissions Requirements

The application process has changed but, in addition, application requirements have evolved. Many universities have made college admissions tests—such as the ACT and SAT—optional for students seeking entry, often with no shortage of internal controversy. In addition, universities have engaged applicants on soft-skill or softer dimensions that move beyond grades and test scores. School-specific essays have become more popular to gauge overall fit.

Enrollment

At a 30,000 foot level, enrollment, broadly, has become more data-driven. Software platforms allow for specific audience targeting and strategic enrollment plans have emphasized specific uses for marketing and recruitment dollars. Applications are accepted earlier in the process, to get students to make a commitment, in hopes of increasing yield. As audience targeting becomes more specific and their messaging better adapts, universities will continue to focus on, and find more success in, recruiting non-traditional students.

Recruitment

Similar to marketing efforts, recruitment has become more specific and less happenstance. Responsive website design, SEO (search engine optimization), web analytics, and the use of CRM (customer relationship management) and CMS (content management system) platforms have become commonplace on most campuses. These new recruitment trends can help establish a more diverse audience and ultimately assist universities in finding students who want a specific degree from a specific institution.

Technology and Recruitment Tools

Many marketing trends are aligned, in some form or fashion, with technology. As such, communication tools and reality-shaping initiatives will continue to be an area of growth and development for institutions. As an emerging trend, we are only seeing the initial ramifications of technology in brand development and marketing for colleges and universities.

Communication Tools
Reality-Shaping Devices

Reality-shaping, or reality-revealing, devices can encourage greater brand awareness. Prospective students tend to enjoy alternative technologies as they engage with their 'hopeful' higher ed world. Virtual reality, both as a recruiting tool and as an innovative pedagogical strategy on campus, has emerged as a formative development. As mentioned above, virtual reality can be used to encourage a new perspective on the campus tour. While not holistic, meaning only a handful of colleges are utilizing VR effectively—or at all—it has still become a formative experience for some colleges. Northern Arizona University, for instance, developed a 360 degree campus tour that has since "invited" 30,000 viewers to their campus. Virtual reailty—immersion in a digitally-created or simulated environment—can bring students to campus no matter their physical location. VR platforms can also be used to encourage donors to give or showcase new and innovative campus projects. Additionally, universities continue to explore VR uses across campus, both within and outside the classroom.

Augmented reality, as a secondary resource, has also become more popular. Augmented reality (AR) will typically superimpose computer-generated images on a user's view of the real-world. AR is popular in applications like Facebook, Instagram and Snapchat. Savannah College of Art and Design (SCAD) not only incorporated VR into their recruiting technique—they provided Google Cardboard to all prospective students—but they also developed a course catalog that provided videos of students' creative sessions and games they designed within individual classes.

Retention

While brand and marketing initiatives bring students to campus, retention efforts keep them present and active. Retention, across the industry, has become a trending concept, gaining truly global attention. In 2014, the University Innovation Alliance was developed to encourage competing institutions to share retention rates with the overarching goal of improvement. The initiative, at the time, was more conversational but it illustrated a crucial point: all institutions, public or private, must engage broadly and intentionally about retention measures and, more specifically, about student success.

Retention efforts start with targeting and yielding best-fit students. But, after institutions get best-fit students to campus, they can build and leverage structures to reinforce student success. One best-fit marketing technique is the reminder to students that their experience will be personalized. Specialized and personal academic and career advising have penetrated institutional structure and new advising models that enhance success will become more commonplace.

Technology and automation—concepts that have shaped marketing and branding measures—will continue to define and refine student retention. For instance, one emerging trend for many colleges is an investment in software that enables personalized advising and course planning. New core systems that track student data and success measures (i.e. key performance metrics) have replaced traditional, and sometimes archaic, student information systems. CRM (Customer relationship management) systems allow institutions to create individualized student profiles that correlate performance indicators to the individual student and larger collections of data as well. The evolution of student information systems has also created a desire for, and means to collect, big data that incorporates predictive analytics. There is a renewed emphasis on automation and mobile technology that allows students to also take control of their course and college experience.

Conclusion

Universities are in a marketing arms race. The initiatives and strategies mentioned above are exciting, but they can be expensive. In a shrinking client market, with increased competition, institutions would be wise to focus intentionally on their marketing efforts. It will not be enough to have a university-driven social presence; instead, institutions must focus on stories and identify influencers who can take the narrative further and push the institution's mission out to a broader audience. The market has changed, but audience desires have changed as well. Prospective students receive information from colleges differently than generations past. The emphasis on individualized recruitment and best-fit strategies are drastically different from the "cast a wide net" strategies of the past. Correspondingly, institutions recognize that retention measures are almost as important as enrollment numbers and, as a result, individual experiences have been trending. Overall, universities must focus on brand recognition and brand loyalty in a market that continues to see volatile market shifts.

Ponder

What innovative marketing techniques does your institution use?

_____
_____
_____
_____
_____
_____
_____
_____

Can you identify or describe your institution's branding philosophy?

How can your institution improve its marketing efforts?

References

Grossman, D. (2013, November 01). Marketing higher education: A historical perspective. Retrieved from https://evolllution.com/opinions/marketing-higher-education-historical-perspective/

Smith, A. & Anderson, M. (2018, March 1). Social media use in 2018. Retrieved from https://www.pewinternet.org/2018/03/01/social-media-use-in-2018/

Section II
Student Services

By James D. Breslin

Student Services

Student Engagement Strategies

From first-year orientation to senior week, those who work on college campuses are almost constantly presented with opportunities to engage students in the life of academe. Between these two seminal experiences, myriad curricular and co-curricular engagement opportunities are offered: summer bridge programming, first-year experience courses, transition support services, academic services, residence hall programming, undergraduate research, service and leadership positions, and on-campus employment opportunities. Though the list is long and varied, many of the principles behind these practices are rooted in a basic understanding of student learning and development. This section offers a brief overview of these foundations, suggestions for how to engage the contemporary college student (while acknowledging that this is not nor has it ever been a monolithic population), and perspectives on engagement for the 21st century learner.

Foundations of Engagement

If you've seen the 1992 film *School Ties*, you already have a sense of much of the history of American higher education, as described by Matt Damon's character Charlie Dillon: "good grades, the right schools, right colleges, the right connections. Those are the keys to the kingdom…We do the things they tell us to do and then they give us the good life." Simple as it is, this sense of higher education, rooted in the white, male, hegemonic culture in which it was developed, is an essentialized description of the function of American higher education pre-World War II. Institutions served white, wealthy, and mostly male children of those who resided in positions of power and prestige. As a result, simply completing the curriculum and earning the credential was mostly unquestioned. These degrees, rigorous though they might have been, were already bought and paid for.

As the United States moved from this model to the massification of higher education, the notion of a postsecondary credential as a public good took hold (Horowitz, 1987; Thelin, 2004). As the myriad, recursive efforts for equal rights aligned with this evolution, and higher education in the 1960s moved away from the *in loco parentis* model, national attention began to focus on who was and who was not completing a degree.

One upshot of this work was the development of theories of student engagement, developed initially by Astin (1984). While there are many outgrowths of this work, both in theory and practice, they have been too-often bottom-lined with a simple precept that has been repeated by Deans of Students, Vice Presidents for Student Affairs, and many other practitioners: "keep them busy, keep them here." This notion of student engagement is as outdated as it is misguided. Reducing the concept of student engagement to keeping students occupied dismisses several decades of theory and practice, the practical notions of which are presented below.

Engaging the 21st Century Student

As students are increasingly accessing higher education primarily to obtain good jobs, the notion of higher education as a public good has begun to erode and positive public perception of higher education increasingly falls on party lines (Pew Research Center, 2017). These shifting perceptions of higher education and the increased politicization of the field and our work creates new challenges, particularly for institutions that are historically quite slow in reacting to emerging trends and issues.

One clear change that has emerged from this evolution is the need to find new ways to foster student engagement on campus and/or online. While we hold that studies around generational trends often result in reports that are over-generalized and too stereotypical to be truly inclusive and intersectional, the conversations in the field around supporting millennial students for the last 10-15 years have illuminated just how much we have to be aware of the continually shifting needs to student populations. For example, in an attempt to engage students who seem to be increasingly invested in their community and larger society, notions of student volunteerism have evolved into community engagement.

From Volunteerism to Social Responsibility

In campus student engagement work, this shift may be evident in the changes witnessed in student volunteer events as part of new student orientations. Similarly, centers for student activities, sustainability, and/or social responsibility have also modified how they do their work. Professionals in these areas have come to understand that students are no longer interested simply in accruing a certain amount of volunteer experience. Rather, they have created comprehensive learning experiences, sometime tied to a formal credit-bearing course, that situates volunteer experiences as one component in a larger effort to foster community-based learning.

This sense that we need to provide students with more community engagement and social understanding in order to engage them has permeated much of the co-curriculum. We have observed that increasingly study abroad opportunities are tied not only to course content rooted in a particular geographical locale, but to the social issues, politics, or other realities of the people who occupy those places.

We hear students talk about wanting more "practical" experiences and skills from their college work, and while that construct can be interpreted in many different ways, we suggest here that students are using that language to tell us that they believe that engaging with a community beyond the confines of the campus and that doing so in deep, meaningful ways provides them with a skillset they desire and believe will be beneficial to them once they graduate. This assertion is supported by data from the employers' perspective as well (Hart, 2010).

Overreliance on Residential Programming

Another outcome of the increased external pressure on higher education and a complicated economic recovery since the Great Recession has been the way the students and increasingly their families evaluate the value proposition of a college education. The traditional ideal of living on campus while attending a four-year institution is being supplanted by increasing questions about the costs of tuition, room and board, and optional programming or experiences.

In the past few decades, higher education institutions have relied heavily on residence life-based programming to foster student engagement on campus. However, given the context cited above, students are increasingly choosing to begin their postsecondary careers at two-year institutions, which rarely have residential facilities, are transferring from one institution to another in significant numbers, and are choosing to commute from home or live off campus to try to decrease out-of-pocket expenses. While residence life operations and staff continue to have a monumental impact on those students who live on campus, there is often a relative dearth of similar resources expended to try to engage students who do not adhere to such a traditional path.

Engaging students in college cannot continue its overreliance on residence hall programming. Practitioners need to think about and experiment with ways to engage students who commute or otherwise live off campus. This sort of engagement work is also too often seen as disconnected from the curriculum and co-curriculum. We believe that higher education still employs an additive approach when trying to foster student engagement and that such a model is outdated and ineffective for current student populations. Rather than jockeying for students' time and trying to get them to commit to one more activity/experience, practitioners should work strategically and collaboratively with colleagues across campus. This might look like colleagues convening to determine which events or activities are most prescient based on student needs and collaborating (rather than competing) to foster engagement. Such an approach can help students situate these experiences as critical and central to their success and part of the academic learning they do in college.

Multidisciplinary and Faculty-Staff Partnerships Matter

In addition to situating student engagement as central to both student learning and success, it is clear that effective strategies include collaborative rather than competitive approaches. Students are not interested in the territoriality or political nature of the different employment roles or hierarchies on a college campus. In fact, they often refer to any university employee as part of the "administration."

Rather than a series of one-off engagement opportunities vying for their time, we suggest that students will be more eager to engage when we can show them how the opportunities available to them in various areas complement each other and can contribute to their success, both during and after college. We encourage faculty and staff to work collaboratively to create plans for timely graduation that are not reduced to a list of courses required to complete a degree. Such planning work should, from the outset, co-locate curricular and co-curricular opportunities. Students are highly motived to complete a degree, and we know engaged students are more likely to finish a postsecondary credential in a timely manner, so aligning these efforts is of mutual benefit.

Student Engagement in a Post-Obama, Post-Truth World

The world has changed rapidly in many ways since the political turmoil that erupted in the United States in 2016, and we would be remiss not to address here how we're beginning to see these changes impact student engagement. The analyses and recommendations here are very new. As of this writing, there has scarcely been sufficient time for higher education researchers to conduct and publish rigorous scholarship on these impacts, but it seems nearly self-evident that these times and issues are creating further change in how we can best foster student engagement.

Politics on Campus

While we discuss political engagement itself elsewhere, the interplay of politics and campus life have a particular impact on student engagement. In general, we believe that most students do want to understand and engage in discourse around the current political landscape, but we also understand that doing so can be very challenging because of the vitriolic rhetoric that can permeate these discussions. We encourage practitioners to consider how to incorporate political dialogue into existing structures and practices on campus, including those that foster engagement with the larger community, connect to issues of public policy, and relate to larger geopolitical and economic realities. Students do seem to want to engage on these issues, and to try to make sense of them in the current environment, but may be wary of misspeaking, causing a backlash, or being the victim of violence, symbolic or physical.

Food and Housing Insecurity

Waves of recent research on higher education demonstrate how narrowly focused the field has traditionally been when trying to understand students' lives. A stark example here is the recent work around both food and housing insecurity among college students. After an initial study that focused solely on students at two-year institutions, a more recent study includes those at four-year institutions as well and found that more than one third of students had experienced food or housing insecurity within 30 days prior to completing the study's survey (Goldrick-Rab, Richardson, Schneider, Hernandez, & Cady, 2018).

This reality of the student experience, across institutional types, sent shockwaves through some parts of the field. The upshot is that administrators and policymakers are increasingly forced to recognize that students' lives do not stop when they leave campus and that these issues have real, profound impacts. Practitioners need to consider how notions of student engagement might be broadened to include issues of effective or equitable access, in essence asking, "what concerns do we need to help ameliorate so that students can engage in higher education?"

Ponder

What offices, positions, and resources might need to collaborate or otherwise align their efforts to support the engagement of the growing number of students who are on less traditional paths through higher education?

_____
_____
_____
_____
_____
_____
_____
_____

What would it look like on your campus if faculty and staff worked together to create a strategic plan for student outreach and engagement throughout each year?

_____
_____
_____
_____
_____
_____
_____
_____

What role does political discourse play in your work with students? How does it relate to your institution's mission?

_____
_____

Does your institution have a sense of its political climate, data on student food and housing insecurity, and other key metrics in order to support effective decision making around student engagement?

References

Astin, A. W. (1984). Student involvement: A developmental theory for higher education. *Journal of College Student Personnel, 25*, 297-308.

Goldrick-Rab, S., Richardson, J., Schneider, J., Hernandez, A., & Cady, C. (2018). Still hungry and homeless in college. *Wisconsin HOPE Lab. Available online: http://wihopelab. com/publications/Wisconsin-HOPE-Lab-Still-Hungry-and-Homeless. pdf (accessed on 25 July 2018)*.

Hart, P. (2010). Raising the bar: Employers' views on college learning in the wake of the economic downturn. A survey among employers conducted on behalf of The Association of American Colleges and Universities by Hart Research Associates: Inc.

Horowitz, H. L. (1987). *Campus Life: Undergraduate Cultures from the End of the Eighteenth Century to Present*. Chicago: The University of Chicago Press.

Pew Research Center. (2017). *Sharp Partisan Divisions in Views of National Institutions: Republicans Increasingly Say Colleges Have Negative Impact on U.S.* Retrieved from www.pewresearch.org

Thelin, J. R. (2004). *A History of American Higher Education*. Baltimore: The Johns Hopkins University Press.

Student Services
Space and Facilities

While we often speak of contested spaces in the field of higher education, there are few spaces as contested as the actual, physical spaces on our campuses. The physical spaces we tend to occupy in higher education often seem special because they are, in fact, relatively uncommon. Not quite the same as educational spaces at other levels, not really the same as most work environments, and particularly prone to petty politics, campus spaces and facilities are core to students' experiences in higher education.

Ask someone on a college campus what a space is used for, and there's a decent chance that the answer will vary significantly based on the respondent. For those of us who have made careers of working in higher education, we tend to think of these facilities with regard to their primary functions: office buildings as faculty/staff spaces, residence halls as student spaces, classrooms as where the magic/test/nap happens, and so on. However, the savvy administrator knows that students experience, occupy, and utilize campus facilities in many ways we never intend, design for, or could even imagine.

We knew in higher education several decades ago that greenspace is important on most campuses, often thought of as a space for studying or throwing a frisbee, but it would have been hard to imagine the quidditch matches that started to spring up in the last decade or so. While by no means an exhaustive list or typology, this section explores the many and varied ways campus spaces may be used, contested issues that often surround campus spaces and their use, and some foundational ideas to keep in mind for long-term space planning and facility design, all with a particular focus on students.

Student Utilization of Campus Spaces

While colleges and universities often draw up grand plans for space utilization, build policies and processes to support their spaces, and commit many dollars to maintenance, students often see and experience spaces on campus quite differently from how administrators, faculty, and staff perceive them. For example, in our office buildings on campuses, faculty and staff tend to see common spaces as waiting areas for those who've made appointments, typically between 8a and 5p. Students might see them as some of the best quiet study space on campus in the evenings and on the weekends if the furniture is relatively comfortable and the space isn't as highly trafficked as the campus library. When administrators think about residence hall rooms, the conversations tend to be about students studying, hanging out, sleeping, grooming, etc. Students might look at the same spaces and consider how many people they can fit into one room for a Friday night party or whether they could put all the beds in a suite in one room and use another room as a large living space.

The reality is that students think about and are likely to utilize spaces in far different ways than intended or designed. Moreover, after decades of deferred maintenance on many campuses and master plans that never quite seem to come to fruition, many institutions find themselves using spaces in ways and for purposes they likely never envisioned. Examples here include residence halls that have been converted into office space (and vice versa), food service spaces converted into student services space, storage areas that are now offices or classrooms, etc.

When it comes to student access and use of spaces, it can be helpful to bear in mind what we know about student learning and development. In particular, theory and research tell us that people learn differently and that our campus spaces would do well to reflect such diversity. Some students need very low distraction, while others thrive when there's a buzz in the background. When thinking about space utilization, it's important to consider how spaces might be zoned not just for different kinds of activity, but also for different kinds of learning.

Critical to this conversation is that students' needs evolve rapidly over time. A beautiful new campus building may still be highly functional after its first decade of operation, but if the physical and technological attributes of the space cannot adapt rapidly, it may already be starting to look and feel like a relic of an earlier era. A watchword in campus space planning should be flexibility. Some of our own recent research demonstrates that students thrive when they have the ability to manipulate their own environments to suit their evolving needs. This could certainly mean furniture that is easily moved or reconfigured, but also mobile walls, technology, and amenities.

The bottom line here is that students move through campuses in many different ways and they rarely draw the stark lines between different kinds of activities that we often do as administrators. Questions to ask in the planning of new or refurbished space might include:

- How easy/costly will it be to update technology or other infrastructure?
- How many features can be semi-permanent?
- What do students think of your initial plans (yes, go ask them!)?

Policies, Politics, and Legalities

We would be remiss to address space and facility use on campus without referencing the politics that come with these issues. Many campuses can feel like a land comprised of mini fiefdoms, where certain floors, buildings, or campus areas are "owned" by a particular campus entity (e.g., department, college, or division). Too often, faculty and staff administrators assess their own stature by evaluating and comparing the relative amounts of space they control. This can lead to turf wars, sometimes almost literally, and can create animosity when there is disagreement about where programs, services, or events should be located.

We recommend trying to maintain a focus on the outcomes we all (hopefully) value: student experiences that foster meaningful learning and development, a campus culture that is collegial and inclusive, and a common sense of purpose. These may seem like lofty goals in the midst of a discussion about which department gets to occupy a new building and which gets the basement of a "campus landmark." Given the comments above about being more flexible in how space is planned, some institutions would do well to consider how overall space usage is allocated. For example, perhaps the notion of an entire floor or building as office space is outdated. Planning teams might consider what it would look like for a pod of offices to be adjacent to classroom, study, or social space. Such creative thinking requires many of us to abandon some of our ideological entrenchments, but could result in new partnerships, working environments, and casual interactions.

An area of campus space management that tends to be far more formal is dealing with the policies and politics of who can use which spaces and for what purposes. Public institutions in particular in American higher education have spent the last few decades navigating issues of free speech on campus, often with judicial intervention. While the United States Supreme Court has affirmed the use of so-called time, space, and manner restrictions, the policies that govern campus access and space utilization are often fraught.

As recent events on college and university campuses around the U.S. have shown, the invitation of speakers to campuses, including by student groups, can be a perilous political landscape. On a more conceptual level, these issues stem from a supposed tension between free speech and political correctness. We invite campus administrators to try to push beyond this paradigm and consider how student agency and activism is really changing the conversations about who gets to speak on campus, what artwork or statuary is part of the campus landscape, how facilities are named, etc. Here are some points to consider around these issues on your campus:

- Is there a clear process for deciding who gets to use spaces and for what purposes? And in particular is that process done objectively and without the detriment of viewpoint discrimination?

- Do you clearly communicate to student and to registered student organizations the requirements and responsibilities for using campus spaces?
- Are your policies and processes reviewed on a regular cycle, or are they driven by each emergency that arises?

Aligning Space Allocation and Institutional Values

As mentioned above, space issues on campus can devolve into contests that are more about relationships, politics, and posturing than about institutional effectiveness. Unfortunately, it can be far too easy in these situations to lose sight of the ways that space allocation portrays our institutional values, whether we intend it to or not.

For example, situating a tutoring center in a poorly lit basement, at the end of a long, empty hallway, and behind a heavy metal door that is not permitted to be propped open, communicates a very clear message about the extent to which such academic support is valued on a particular campus (NB: this is not a hypothetical example). On the other hand, locating an office of multicultural affairs in the midst of a student center, adjacent to a major artery for foot traffic on campus, and with transparent and updated space, portrays a very different message.

Beyond optics, these decisions communicate our institutional priorities, whether we want to acknowledge it or not. Highly effective institutions and their leaders will recognize that conversations about facilities and space cannot easily be divorced from discussions of mission, efficacy, and strategic planning. While the design and management of campus physical space may be situated in a particular office or division, the work of continually remaking our campuses cannot be so siloed.

Further, while a sense is emerging in the field that the "amenities race" of the last 15 or so years is waning, we want to clarify here that we are not suggesting that institutions must have the newest, shiniest spaces in order to be competitive or serve students effectively. Indeed, careful campus planning that keeps spaces relatively fresh, even when they've been serving the institution for decades, can be quite attractive not just for prospective students and employees, but for engaging current enrolled students.

Master Planning, Capital Projects, and Universal Design

It is not uncommon in higher education to hear faculty and staff bemoan campus master planning processes as pipe dreams, unrealistic, or fait accompli. There are many reasons why a plan that spans multiple decades is unlikely to ever come to fruition as it was originally conceived. Even if we dismiss all the new trends and issues that emerge in such a timespan, there are fiscal realities that continually impact these efforts.

This said, master planning serves a number of important functions in the day-to-day life of an institution. There can be a sense of continuity when these plans transcend the ideas and leaders of a particular moment, and they can help garner a sense of institutional commitment and pride. Moreover, a clear master plan that details when new facilities will be built, and old spaces refurbished, can help mitigate the political squabbling referenced above regarding who gets to occupy what spaces and for what purposes.

It is critical to consider who is at the master planning table for such aims to be achieved. To wit, these are not conversations that should be shrouded in secrecy or only shared among executive leaders and board members. Rather, master planning committees should include both faculty and staff at various levels, as well as student representatives and possibly even community members. This inclusive approach from the beginning allows each constituent group to provide input through its representative(s) and helps build a shared sense of purpose that can transcend crises of the moment.

Capital Projects and Private-Sector Partnerships

Capital projects in particular often become high-stakes affairs on college campuses. While some larger institutions are building continuously, such trends are on the decline as steadily declining birth rates over the last two decades are resulting in decreases of traditional college-going populations. In an effort to circumnavigate the resource scarcity that can result from these trends and also keep pace with each other, institutions increasingly turn to partnerships with the private sector for construction efforts.

There are now myriad examples of such partnerships and they transcend institutional types and tiers. Often highly customized and somewhat secretive, partnerships with private corporations offer the allure of new facilities with little or no upfront cost to the institution. However, as such agreements are relatively new and are designed to last for decades (e.g., a fifty-year land lease is often standard for a new residence hall), there are many unanswered questions, both practical and legal, that come from these contractual agreements. Of course, institutional leaders should rely on their counsel to advise them on such matters, and we make no such claims here.

There are more conceptual questions arise for higher education professionals. What happens to such facilities when the land lease ends and, presumably, the facility has essentially reached the end of its usable life? Some professionals have referred to some such facilities as "disposable," which raises a host of ethical questions. In the coming years, institutions will have to begin planning for the end of these contracts, make decisions about how they will support maintenance of the legacy facilities, or explore further partnerships to refurbish or replace them.

Universal Design as an Equity Issue

At this point, nearly all American higher education institutions have made some claim to inclusion, equity, or social justice. While these efforts often manifest themselves in new academic programs, structural supports for students, or reviews of labor practices for employees, they also intersect with campus facility construction and management. It can no longer be acceptable for an institution to build a new facility or refurbish an existing one without considering accessibility as a core equity issue.

It was not uncommon even ten years ago to hear institutional leaders bemoan the addition of a ramp to a building exterior as an added cost or eyesore. Current trends both in American society and higher education require all constituents involved in these projects to center the needs, both current and anticipated, of all individuals who will use them. Certainly, this includes physical access issues like ramps (or grading land so that there are no steps at all), automated doors, and elevators. As awareness has increased of the need to acknowledge and respect trans people and their needs, discussions about restrooms, signage, residence hall policies, information system fields, and many other areas must be examined (see for example Squire & Beck, 2016).

These are but two examples of the sorts of needs that administrators must consider, budget for, and be intentional around. Principles of universal design should be foundational to space planning conversations. These discussions are most effective when they transcend the minimum requirements as established by current laws and regulations and actually focus on the current and anticipated needs of all people. Far from being an afterthought, centering these principles is a key way that institutions can live their commitment to equity and inclusion.

Ponder

What do you know about space planning, allocation, and maintenance on your campus?

_____
_____
_____
_____
_____
_____
_____

Who was included in the design of the most recent space you developed?

_____
_____
_____
_____
_____
_____
_____

How often does your institution review policies around space allocation and utilization?

_____
_____
_____
_____
_____
_____
_____

Can you locate your campus master plan in less than five minutes? What does your response mean?

_____
_____
_____
_____
_____
_____
_____

References

Squire, D., & Beck, B. (2016). *Developmental Pathways to Trans Inclusion on College Campuses*. ACPA—College Student Educators International, Washington, D.C.

Student Services

The Student Experience

Even as retention and graduation rates have become the currency of the realm, the myriad benefits many students enjoy from their time in higher education emanate from the overall experience. As institutions have abandoned the *in loco parentis* doctrine that permeated the first half of the twentieth century in higher education, the need to understand, craft, support, and assess the comprehensive student experience on our campuses has never been more important.

While we promote initiatives like "15 to finish," and talk to students about how to manage their time, we have a tendency in higher education to fall into the trap of thinking of students' time and experiences as existing in discrete categories. If we are willing to understand the student experience holistically, and to reframe the curriculum as something that is communicated not just in classrooms and laboratories (Nespor, 1990), then it becomes clear that we have vast opportunities to foster student learning and development. This section explores the places, structures, and processes for understanding the student experience from matriculation to graduation.

Experiences in the Curricular Spectrum

With the explicit, appropriate focus on the formal coursework students encounter, it can be easy for those who work in higher education to lose sight of the fact that students typically only spend about 15 hours per week in the classroom or lab. For so-called traditional students who matriculate to institutions directly from high school, this is almost the inverse of their previous educational experiences. We expect them to transition from having their time highly structured, regulated, and planned for them, to having near total autonomy over their time and educational experiences. Other students who are entering higher education with more life experience may sometimes be unaware that relatively few hours per week in the classroom does not translate to relatively little time that needs to be budgeted for academic work in a given week. This temporal component is, of course, only one dimension of the transitions students experience when they begin their higher education.

While the traditional understanding of the curriculum as something that is discrete, facilitated only by faculty, and that only happens in certain places is as outdated as it is inaccurate, it is still a prevailing paradigm in higher education. Conceptualized here more as a continuum, the sections that follow explore the dimensions of the student experience throughout the curriculum.

The Formal Curriculum

Remember MOOCs and how they were going to "change everything" about higher education? It seems clear that what was heralded as a disruptive revolution and THE way of the future has fizzled in many ways. However, that does not mean that the formal curriculum in higher education has not changed and does not continue to change. While those reticent to embrace change may look at the last 10-15 years in higher education and learn that digging in, burying one's head in the proverbial sand, and waiting for the latest fad to blow over is an effective strategy, the history of higher education shows us that the curriculum does change and that it needs to continue to do so.

Different content delivery methods and strategies are continuing to emerge, and we seem to only be at the very beginning of this evolution. Online platforms, resources, and tools have absolutely changed how we deliver educational content in postsecondary education. Like other curricular shifts, though, this change happens somewhat gradually. There is every reason to expect that the continued development of smart, connected devices, predictive analytics, and AI will continue to shape how we "do" the traditional curriculum in higher education.

Moreover, the formal curriculum has often been painfully slow to acknowledge and adapt to evolving student needs or the vast and expanding understanding of student learning in the field. As traditional-age college-going populations are forecast to decline over the next 25 years, faculty and academic administrators will be faced with increasing competition across institutions and heightened calls for curricula that adapt to student needs more quickly. This part of the student experience is critical. While students by no means see their coursework as disconnected from other experiences on campus, they are increasingly aware of how they learn and the need to advocate for themselves. This should not be confused as the same concerns many had in the 1990s about student consumerism. The two issues may manifest in similar ways at times, but they are different.

Another emerging trend in recent student populations is a growing understanding that equity, inclusion, and full participation are not empty rhetoric, nor are they merely watchwords of social activism. Students increasingly express concerns about equity in learning spaces, including the formal curriculum. Students often expect to engage in difficult conversations, not just with each other, but also with their faculty. This can be intimidating to some instructors, particularly when there might be credible concern about being "put on blast" via YouTube, Instagram, or Snapchat. That being said, moving forward students will expect institutions to present material from different perspectives, cultures, and histories not as anachronistic examples or asides, but as core to the learning they are expected to do.

This is part of a larger trend in what students want from their experience in higher education: deep, meaningful, and impactful relationships with faculty. To be sure, students are still likely to find faculty intimidating, and they readily recognize the expertise that faculty possess. However, they also expect that faculty show up at important events, engage in dialogue about current events, and connect course content to the real world. When it comes to conversations about equity, power, oppression, or marginalization, students do not expect faculty to have all the answers. However, they do expect their instructors to be "in it" with them, to embrace the messy, challenging conversations, and to acknowledge the tensions that exist in contemporary society.

The Co-Curriculum

This part of the continuum of student experiences in higher education consists of those programs, services, and opportunities on campus that have some connection to students' formal learning, but that exist outside the classroom. This can include services that have been prevalent in higher education for hundreds of years, such as tutoring or writing support, as well as programmatic initiatives like those found in learning communities, residence halls, centers for student engagement, offices of multiculturalism or inclusion, and the like.

While there is a tendency in higher education to conceptualize these spaces and experiences as supplemental to formal coursework, we find it clear that there is sufficient research on the impacts of these opportunities to understand them as connected learning enterprises in their own right. These kinds of co-curricular contexts are spaces where students' academic and social lives intersect, often vibrantly. For example, engaging in small group discussion in a peer tutoring context is not simply a way for students to better understand their chemistry homework. The powerful social dynamic, which is integral to effective learning and development, means that students are learning new skills and approaches, developing schemas for having academic conversation with their peers, and rehearsing the role of what it means to be an effective college student.

Moreover, when substantive student learning happens outside the classroom, it would be foolhardy to dismiss such student opportunities as incidental, minor, or secondary. Higher education becomes most effective when faculty and staff work with a genuine esprit de corps, recognizing that the holistic learning (sum) of students' experiences is far greater than the individual outcomes in separate spaces.

A practical example for how staff and faculty colleagues might achieve such aims is to collaborate on student learning outcomes mapping at an institutional level. For a variety of reasons, including accreditation and compliance, most student-facing units at any given institution will have a set of student learning outcomes that have been maintained, assessed, and updated regularly. Faculty and staff can work collaboratively to map the outcomes from a general education curriculum, a major curriculum, and co-curricular experiences to help understand if their efforts are working in concert or are just creating a cacophony of confusion for their students.

Finally, it merits attention that the individuals who create co-curricular opportunities for students play an integral role in the life of an institution and in the academic success of its students. These professionals should be selected with care, situated where they can access and impact centers of power on campus, and be expected to engage in the intellectual life of the institution.

Institutional Services

It can be far too easy for administrators and campus leaders to overlook the experiences students have with institutional services. Whether it's the nuts and bolts of a course registration or degree audit system, the process to apply for and procure a parking permit, or what happens when a student living in a residence hall submits a maintenance request, these seemingly-straightforward processes are absolutely part of students' overall experience in our institutions.

Further, these are also experiences that are ripe for student learning and development. The prevailing paradigm in the field is to conceptualize students' experiences with institutional services on a continuum that ranges from "purely bureaucratic/a real pain" to "customer services focused and easy to get what they want." Professionals in the field often cite examples of how they have identified supposed barriers to student persistence, such as parking, complicated scholarship applications, or slow responses from IT support services and have worked with those units on campus to get students what they need as simply as possible.

While there is merit to understanding how these experiences can serve as barriers, it also is worth considering how these processes can support student learning. In an era where there are constant memes, Twitter accounts, and email forwards that poke fun at "millennial students," and when students increasingly seem to request "life skills" as a need on their campuses, it is reasonable to try to disrupt the paradigm above and look for ways to make students' experiences with institutional services both effective and educational.

Examples of this work might include financial aid offices that have partnered with colleagues on and off campus to provide students with some education regarding financial literacy. Perhaps a dining services unit could provide a limited number of cooking classes included in the price of a semester meal plan. These are but two examples of how this approach could be implemented. The overarching point is that the development of process delivery outcomes is as critical for institutional services as student learning outcomes are to academic programs.

Framing Online Experiences as a Seamless Part of the Student Experience

We would be remiss not to acknowledge the profound and pervasive ways that students' online and digital experiences in higher education are part of their holistic learning. This is true as much for students who participate in-person on campus as it is for those who only ever attend remotely. Much as we call above for process delivery outcomes and student learning outcomes for on-campus experiences, the same attention must be paid to students' online experience.

Further, higher education must work to understand how students' use of technology evolves over time and does so rapidly. While there are platforms, such as our institutional ERPs and

LMSs that essentially function as ecosystems that faculty and staff can design and manipulate, student use of private sector tools and media can help us assess and meet their needs. A contemporary example here is the way that many faculty and staff are currently working to engage students on Facebook. Just so we're all on the same page: they aren't really using Facebook! Try Instagram or Snapchat.

Institutions would do well to assess what kinds of interactions are most important to and impactful for students in different spaces. For example, it's certainly possible to hold a Snapchat-based advising session. However, if students are not looking for advising on social media and not interested in accessing it there, then such an effort would be a waste of time and resources. Higher education professionals and administrators must work to develop a robust, regularly-updated understanding of where, how, and when to provide various experiences rather than simply throwing everything at students all the time.

The Student Experience and Their Continual Evaluation of the Value Proposition

The myriad pressures on higher education, the increasing acerbic political rhetoric, and rapidly evolving student needs are only some of the reasons that students, their families, and other supporters continue to question the value of a higher education. Meanwhile, most institutions operate under the dated paradigm that we simply need to convince students to pick our institution during the admissions process and keep them engaged in order for them to persist and graduate. Now more than ever, students are evaluating the value proposition of their particular college or university and they do so well beyond the admissions process.

National data shows that well more than a third of all students who matriculate to a four-year institution will transfer to another institution at least once (Shapiro et al., 2018). While students cite countless reasons for choosing to transfer, we know that they typically take the totality of their experience into account when making these decisions. An institution that is committed to graduating critical, engaged citizens must also be committed to fostering and assessing a student experience that connects educational opportunities across the vast expanse of students' interactions with the institution, to attending to students' diverse needs and interests, and to understanding that students' perceptions of their institution are formed by their evaluation of their *whole* experience and not just the discrete parts.

Ponder

How does your institution craft a curriculum for students? Who is at the table?

_____
_____
_____
_____
_____
_____
_____

How do you and your institution make sense of the curriculum and co-curriculum?

_____
_____
_____
_____
_____
_____
_____

What might it look like from the student perspective to evaluate the relative value of attending your institution *throughout* the student lifecycle?

References

Nespor, J. (1990). Curriculum and conversions of capital in the acquisition of disciplinary knowledge. *Journal of Curriculum Studies, 22*(3), 217-232.

Shapiro, D., Dundar, A., Huie, F., Wakhungu, P. K., Bhimdiwali, A., Nathan, A., & Youngsik, H. (2018). *Transfer and Mobility: A National View of Student Movement in Postsecondary Institutions, Fall 2011 Cohort*. Retrieved from National Student Clearinghouse.

Student Services
Career Development

"Jobs." That's the first, and often the second and third answer when you ask students, their families, and other stakeholders about why higher education is important and worth funding with both public and private dollars. In a public policy and political context where higher education is supposed to serve as a local and regional economic engine, questions about placement and career readiness are already pervasive in the field. Curiously, these conversations often seem to be separated from discussions about student debt, increasing aid, and the nature of higher education as a public good.

Regardless, career development plays an increasingly prominent role for all colleges and universities. While career development and job placement are at the forefront of so many conversations about higher education, administrators are often called upon to help set and square expectations, expand understanding, and connect the dots for many constituents. This section discusses current issues in career development, their connections to institutional priorities, and considerations for higher education professionals.

That's Not My Job

The notion that college or university personnel are not responsible for career readiness is both outdated and fails to align with stakeholder expectations, both internal and external to institutions. This reality does not and should not reduce higher education to job training. In fact, such oversimplification would be counterproductive when research shows that a student completing a bachelor's degree today will have held 13 different jobs by the midpoint of their working lives. That is a radical departure from the realities of work for recent generations.

As such, faculty and staff should not be expected to perform simple job training, but to prepare students for multiple careers in their decades after graduation. This requires redirecting questions like "how will this course/material help me do my job" to "here is how this course/material will prepare you for a lifetime of contributing to society in this area." For several decades higher education has essentially relied on parents, their benefactors, and public funding to trust that the skills, knowledge, and abilities accrued in a degree program are worth both the individual and public investment. For many reasons, that seemingly straightforward part of our social contract has been called into question, resulting in a weakened national educational system.

In addition to wanting a relatively secure financial future, students today are also interested in how they will contribute to their future communities. Combining these aims provides fertile ground for creating new degree programs or refreshing those that are stale from many years of incremental change. Moreover, the desire for career readiness and job placement provides an opportunity for higher education leaders to demonstrate just how valuable and central our institutions are to the present and future success of our societies.

Careers, Gen Eds, and the Liberal Arts

So often students ask why they have to take "all these gen eds" while faculty make painstaking alternations to such requirements, often rooted in the liberal arts tradition from which nearly all American higher education emanates. Students questioning these core requirements are often dismissed in higher education, but they provide us a critical opportunity: a chance to help students understand the value of a more holistic education in a meaningful way.

We have good research (Hart, 2010) demonstrating that a liberal arts education builds exactly the kinds of skills employers cite as core to new employee success. We also know that academic programs provide students both a deep dive into a particular discipline and a set of ways to make sense of the world around them.

Thus, career readiness is not just about completing a degree and the ability to construct an effective résumé and cover letter. We have to take responsibility for helping students understand the whole spectrum of what they learn in college is valuable to them and can inform their work. Leaders in this work will be clear and explicit with students about the outcomes of a general education course or curriculum and help them understand that these skills make them both more critical citizens and more attractive prospective employees.

Who Should Career Services Serve?

Put simply, higher education leaders must help shift the mindset that a career center is a place for those in their final year who are looking for a job. These units have become central to helping students work through a discernment process to determine what kind of work actually fits with their skills, values, and interests. This often requires students to face a harsh reality, namely that they may no longer be interested in the job or career they have long looked forward to. Students need support in these moments as they share with friends and family that their path seems to have shifted.

For students who are returning to higher education or who have been in the workforce already, this process can feel even more high stakes. Such students are often all too well aware of the cost of higher education, and the notion of deviating from a carefully constructed plan can feel overwhelming. Regardless of where they are in their individual lives, time on a college campus, however long the degree program, is an opportunity for students to gain a clear understanding of what credential they really want and how it can most benefit them.

To wit, career services should serve students in each phase of their education. Well-trained professionals in this area can help cross-train admissions and recruitment staff so that these individuals can help prospective students have realistic expectations while they are making decisions about where to enroll. Such offices are now central to helping students prepare for, identify, obtain, and make the most of internship opportunities. On a more conceptual level, career services professionals can help students synthesize their various experiences in higher education, on and off campus, so that they can both develop a more comprehensive understanding of what they have learned and create a robust narrative for future employers about how they can contribute to an organization's success.

Interconnectedness of Academic and Career Advising

Given that there is a place for career services in each phase of the student lifecycle, there are clear connections between academic and career advising. While each field is important in its own right, good collaboration between the two can lead to more beneficial outcomes for students. Cross-training can be an optimal way for both academic and career advisors to have a sense of what students are getting from each service, identify and fill any gaps, and share a coherent narrative with students regarding how to maximize their time in college.

Professionals who have worked in both fields will recognize that it can be a new level of awareness as students discover there are entire fields and professions that were previously unknown to them. Indeed, many of us working in higher education today were likely unaware of the myriad opportunities in this field when we first began our own college or university experience. Students in most programs and most institutional types will benefit from some sort of discernment process.

The goal of this work should not be to convince students on choosing a particular path. Instead, we should be nudging students to explore why a particular path is the best fit for them, how it helps them achieve their long-term goals, and if it will provide them with a sense of purpose in their lives (if that's what they desire from their work). Some implementations of these efforts have taken the form of meta majors, where students select from five or six disciplinary areas, not necessarily arranged by college or school on a given campus, and are advised into a pathway for the variety of individual majors in that area. This approach allows students an opportunity to explore a number of different potential fields while also having a clear path to timely graduation regardless of which they ultimately choose. This sort of creative restructuring of academic pathways will likely become more common as the pressure intensifies for higher education to connect learning outcomes and career readiness.

Career Advising as Central to the Work of Staff and Faculty

The kinds of efforts described above should help make it clear that career advising is central to the work of both faculty and staff in higher education. Faculty have a responsibility to keep their curricula relevant, informed by current trends and issues in their fields, and applicable in today's environment. Faculty should be eager to help students understand what it's like to work in their field and to help them make important connections across disciplines.

While career services and academic advising staff responsibilities are described above, many staff on campuses have responsibilities that help students achieve career readiness. Perhaps the best example here is around student employment. Whether funded via federal or state work study programs or by institutional dollars, many students engage in on-campus work, often from their very first term at an institution. Those who supervise students in these roles have a real responsiblity to take these positions seriously.

While student-staff may be necessary just to make an office on campus function, staff who supervise them should help students understand how their work contributes to the success of the unit. Moreover, these supervisors can have a profound influence on how students approach their work, the ways they learn to hold themselves accountable, and how they learn new skills on the job. Practical implementation can be as simple as requiring students to submit a formal resumé with their application, go through an interview process, and have students sign an employment contract that outlines their responsibilities. Effective leaders in this area will require that student-staff undergo performance evaluations and include them in decision- and policy-making processes. Further, those on the leading edge of this work will consider new paradigms that situate student-staff as colleagues (Breslin, Kope, O'Hatnick, & Sharpe, 2018).

Engaging Key Constituents

Finally, career development on campus is an outstanding opportunity to engage constituents in creative ways. Higher education administrators should consider how they can leverage relationships with all external constituents to benefit all parties. A straightforward example are alumni. These individuals often maintain a connection to the institution, can benefit from ongoing career services, and can serve as mentors or connectors for current students.

Given the intense rhetoric from politicians and government leaders about the need for higher education to drive local economies, administrators should establish contacts in local and regional government and be willing to make specific requests. These could be as simple as internship or co-op opportunities for students, but might also include resource allocation, speaking engagements on campus, or community partnerships. These efforts can benefit all institutions and provide meaningful opportunities for both current students and alumni.

Finally, administrators should consider how to engage board members and other community leaders who hold leadership positions in companies and local non-profit organizations. Individuals in these roles who have a connection to an institution are often willing to partner, but it is incumbent on higher education professionals to generate some initial ideas and reach out to start a dialogue.

Ponder

How and when do you and your institution help students understand the values of general education and a liberal arts core?

_____
_____
_____

How do you support students once they have decided to transition academic majors? Does it go beyond course scheduling?

How do you provide space for intentional major/career exploration and discernment?

What do you do to ensure faculty and staff are working in concert to promote career readiness?

How can your institution leverage student employment experiences to enhance career readiness across all disciplines?

How are you engaging you constituent groups (e.g., alumni, board members, or community leaders) in fostering career discernment and readiness?

References

Breslin, J. D., Kope, M. H., O'Hatnick, J. L., & Sharpe, A. G. (2018). Students as colleagues: A paradigm for understanding student leaders in academic support. *The Learning Assistance Review, 23*(2), 41-64.

Hart, P. (2010). Raising the bar: Employers' views on college learning in the wake of the economic downturn. A survey among employers conducted on behalf of The Association of American Colleges and Universities by Hart Research Associates: Inc.

Student Services

Advising and Student Guarantees

The concept of academic advising has evolved considerably as higher education, and in particular the academic programs we offer, has become more complex and bureaucratic. Several decades ago, advising may have referred primarily or solely to the need to select and register for particular courses, all in the service of completing a degree on-time. In the intervening years, in addition to increasing bureaucracy, faculty time has become both more highly regimented by the requirements of teaching, research, and service, while simplistic, transactional notions of advising have evolved to much more nuanced understanding of this activity as a high-impact practice for student success.

One result of these shifts is that advising has become a subfield of study and practice all its own, though this is a realization that is still slowly seeping into the consciousness of some higher education leaders. Further, students' needs and the associated expectations for advisors have changed. Students themselves are navigating far more complex institutions while also confronting socio-cultural realities that pull them in many directions. Students are increasingly likely to talk to their advisors about much more than academics, including their disabilities, family or relationship experiences, roommate issues, mental health concerns, and rape or sexual assault, among others.

Faculty, while highly trained in their respective fields of study, may easily find themselves overwhelmed at the range of issues that can arise in a 30-minute advising session. They may also feel out of their depth when students disclose some deeply personal issues, looking to the advisor for an open ear and a willingness to support. The reality is that students today often do not try to compartmentalize their lives the ways students may have attempted to do in the past. Advising practices evolved and students expect, and have a right to expect, some baseline levels of emotional intelligence, knowledge of institutional (not merely academic) policies and resources, and sound counsel.

There are myriad implications for institutions here, as well. For example, the complex network of regulatory compliance issues has requirements around documenting, reporting, and investigating certain kinds of issues when students report them. Such regulations do not typically vary based on *which* employee or type of employee hears the student report. This creates real potential liability issues when advisors are not universally and consistently trained as responsible campus personnel for these purposes. Beyond mere compliance, academic advising can serve to enhance student persistence, thriving, retention, and graduation. As a result, this is an area of practice that few institutions can choose to ignore.

Contemporary Advising Practice

From first-year orientation to senior week, those who work as academic advisors are at the core of students' experiences in higher education. The National Academic Advising Association (NACADA) promotes the concept of advising as an educational practice (2006). As various areas of the co-curriculum have increasingly become outcome-driven and assessed accordingly, advising has been at the forefront of this movement. The concept of the advising syllabus was introduced more than a decade ago and has become a standard practice on many campuses.

This reorientation of advising helps frame this area of practice away from prescriptive, transactional notions of course selection and registration. Instead, contemporary advising practice is rooted in discussions of student learning, setting learning outcomes for the advising experience, creating a series of interactions (in person and online, synchronous and asynchronous) to structure that learning, and regular assessment and continuous improvement. Advisors often serve as guides, supporting students as they navigate institutional structures, policies, and bureaucracies; as interpreters who support students as they learn the lexicon of higher education; and as connectors, ensuring that students are able to access the resources they need when the time arises.

Understood this way, it should be clear that effective, impactful advising is not something that happens in one appointment or conversation each semester. These outcomes can be achieved when sufficient relationships are built, support is supplied, and students are challenged to push the boundaries of their prior learning and expectations. This makes transitions from one advisor to another a pivotal moment, for students and administrators would do well to take great care in how these hand-offs are structured. Advising practices are most effective when students, and in particular their learning and development, are centered in institutional decision-making processes. This can be challenging to institutional and neoliberal norms that tend to center faculty while also prioritizing efficiency.

Emerging Next Practices in Advising

Increasingly, advising is understood not just as an effective transition support as students enter our institutions, but as a highly effective way to support student thriving and persistence to timely graduation. In recent years, professional academic advisors have incorporated student development theory and aspects of positive psychology into their practice; the latter manifests most commonly in appreciative advising (Bloom, Hutson, & He, 2008; Bloom, Hutson, He, & Konkle, 2013). This humanistic approach values the whole student and seeks to support students holistically, rejecting the compartmentalization some more seasoned advisors may long for.

Next practices in advising will continue to center the student in advising work and will increasingly call on advisors to understand and work to supports students' issues beyond the confines of higher education. For example, recent research has demonstrated that many students in higher education institutions, both two- and four-year, regularly experience food and/or housing insecurity (Goldrick-Rab, Richardson, Schneider, Hernandez, & Cady, 2018). Advisors are increasingly confronted with students who may not know where their next meal will come from, do not have a regular place to sleep and bathe, or who do not have access to warm clothes when cold weather sets in.

These issues have been present in higher education in recent decades as there have been efforts to expand access, but too often higher education faculty and staff are painfully unaware of such student realities. The future of advising, and of student success efforts in the field, requires this more holistic understanding of the lived student experience. Moreover, advisors will be called not just to an awareness of these issues, but to help students navigate the resources that can provide support to them.

Institutions might consider a number of initiatives to support their advisors in this phase of their work, beginning with the implementation of rigorous assessment to determine the kinds of issues students are facing. Administrators might consider creating a reserve fund for microgrants that advisors could help funnel to support students for immediate needs. For example, an auto mechanic bill of a few hundred dollars can be the difference between persisting and dropping out for some students, and an advisor may be the only institutional representative with whom a student shares such personal information.

Institutions that foster effective next practices in advising will understand that advisors are at the nexus of the student experiences and are uniquely positioned to impact student success. This will require another revolution in how advisors and their practice are conceptualized in the field. Just as advising has undergone a change from prescriptive to developmental, it must now evolve to be truly holistic and thereby include a dimension of advocacy. Administrators would do well to note that this in no way constitutes coddling students, but instead recognizes their lived reality, humanity, and inherent dignity.

Pie Crust Promises: Student Guarantees

Over the last two decades, generally declining birth rates have resulted in associated declines in traditional age college-going populations in the United States, increasing competition to recruit and retain undergraduate students, among other strategies to diversify revenue streams. Moreover, as the public and political rhetoric has become increasingly caustic around higher education, and financial support from federal and state governments has been increasingly unstable, institutions are under intense pressure to demonstrate that earning a credential on their campus (or via their online learning platform) is worth the associated costs.

In recent years, student guarantees have been introduced as a way to demonstrate this value, but also as a way to reinforce the kinds of high-impact practices that also tend to promote student persistence, success, and graduation. The notion of a guarantee is a relatively new concept in the field, its application or definition is inconsistent, and the actual value of such assurances often unclear. As this section explores, the current state of student guarantees in higher education may best be summarized by what Mary Poppins cheerfully characterized as pie crust promises: easily made and easily broken.

On-time Graduation

As students and their families are more frequently and consistently re-evaluating the value proposition of postsecondary education, the likelihood of graduating "on time" has become an important aspect of their decision making. Of course, completing a credential on time can have varying definitions depending on the type of degree or certificate the student is pursuing. Over the last decade or so, some colleges and universities have worked to mitigate this concern by guaranteeing that a student can complete a bachelor's degree in four years.

Such guarantees are typically highly touted by admissions staff and accompanied by a promise that the institution will pay for additional courses or semesters if a student does not graduate after four years. On its face, this assurance would seem to mollify many students and their families. However, the fine print associated with these guarantees is often designed to ensure that an institution would very rarely be responsible for those costs. Common stipulations for the student in an on-time graduation guarantee might include that a student never fails or needs to repeat a course, that the student never change their major, that a student always follows the prescriptive advice of an academic advisor, or that a student complete a certain number of credit hours per year while maintaining good academic standing.

While these stipulations might seem relatively straightforward, they are carefully crafted to ensure that the institution is providing free coursework only in the rarest of circumstances. In effect, these on-time graduation guarantees are suggesting that if students never encounter significant struggles in their academic careers, are sufficiently privileged to remain enrolled full-time, and have systems of support to allow them to behave in ways the institution deems appropriate, then the student is protected financially from being "misadvised." There are clear issues of privilege and power in these promises in that they are essentially designed to benefit students who are already disproportionately more likely to succeed anyway.

Study Abroad and Internships

In addition to guaranteeing on-time graduation, some colleges and universities have also implemented supplementary guarantees. These are often associated with activities that research shows correlate both with highly impactful student learning and increased marketability or employability post-graduation. Two of the most common examples here are study abroad and internship guarantees.

Again, as students and families are increasingly aware of and making decisions about higher education to benefit their career/ earnings ability, they increasingly understand that internships and study abroad may provide them with an advantage in the marketplace. It is critical to understand these issues through a lens of economic privilege, noting that students who come from upper- and middle-class backgrounds are typically better positioned to afford and have access to internship and study abroad opportunities. Thus, when implemented effectively and supported appropriately, these kinds of guarantees have the potential to include students from marginalized backgrounds who are likely to have less access to such opportunities.

As with the on-time graduation guarantees, institutions tend to include stipulations in the fine print of these guarantees. In particular with things like internships and study abroad, institutions are often guaranteeing the *opportunity* to engage in these activities, not that every student will automatically do so. Students might be required to take and pay for certain additional coursework to prepare them for such experiences, engage in different types of advising or academic counseling to qualify, or meet other requirements. Again, for students who are working less than 20 hours per week, have limited personal obligations, and are relatively stable economically, these may seem like very reasonable requirements. That could be quite different for students who have less privilege and power.

Guarantees as Marketing Tool

As the discussion here lays bare, student guarantees are relatively new tools that institutions have developed. As such, their design and implementation strategies are quite varied. The savvy higher education administrator will take note of where in the field or at an institution such guarantees might be proposed. Often emanating from an admissions or enrollment management office, these kinds of guarantees often originate as a marketing tool.

Even with this acknowledgement, the ability of these guarantees to hold higher education professionals and administrators accountable for student success across all populations suggests that there may be merit in deploying them to help close achievement gaps. The stipulations that institutions have designed can and often are amended, creating an opportunity for institutions who are committed to serving all students to consider how to become more student ready. Future research will provide more insights on any long-term outcomes from the implementation of these guarantees, and whether they might persist in the field for the long-term or be abandoned as a marketing strategy as they become more commonplace, and therefore less of a differentiator as competition for students grows.

Ponder

When did your institution last revise or conduct a program evaluation of its advising model?

How do you measure successful advising interactions beyond satisfaction?

How complicated is the advising experience from the student perspective? Can you map out the process including major milestones on a single sheet of paper?

Have you spoken with your advising team about what sort of conceptual or theoretical models inform their work?

What do you see and hear when you observe the interactions between admissions staff and prospective students/families?

References

Bloom, J. L., Hutson, B. L., & He, D. Y. (2008). *The appreciative advising revolution.* Champaign, IL: Stipes.

Bloom, J. L., Hutson, B. L., He, Y., & Konkle, E. (2013). Appreciative education. *New Directions for Student Services, 2013*(143), 5-18.

Goldrick-Rab, S., Richardson, J., Schneider, J., Hernandez, A., & Cady, C. (2018). Still hungry and homeless in college. *Wisconsin HOPE Lab. Available online: http://wihopelab. com/publications/Wisconsin-HOPE-Lab-Still-Hungry-and-Homeless.pdf (accessed on 25 July 2018).*

National Academic Advising Association. (2006). NACADA concept of academic advising.

Student Services

Social and Political Engagement

It is no secret to higher education professionals and administrators today that student engagement in political and social movements is part of our reality. For those whose first experiences in the field, even as students, were in the 1990s or early 2000s, this may seem like a bit of shift. In those days of relatively stable funding and increasing enrollments, laments of students being apathetic to the world around them were prolific. Now that students have become more engaged in these efforts, as they have been in the past, there have been veritable crises about how campus administrators should react, support, or attempt to limit such activity.

Perceptions and opinions about the connections between social change and higher education are quite diverse, but the fact that, in general, student political engagement has increased over the last century or so should not be a surprise. As student enrollments rose dramatically nationally throughout the twentieth century, American higher education transitioned from educating the children of the truly elite to serving a somewhat more representative proportion of the body politic.

This section explores the more prevalent issues that administrators encounter around student social and political activism and concludes with a challenge to consider what frameworks we use to make sense of this kind of student engagement and how we relate to it. That said, this section is not a legal or regulatory analysis and is not written to provide such counsel. There is no doubt that student engagement and activism do intersect with such concerns, but administrators should always consult their own counsel when they have questions.

Uncomfortable Conversations and Controversial Speakers

Conversations around politics, social justice, and full participation can be fraught with emotions from all participants. As such, administrators must take great care to remember that students are engaging in activism while they are also in the midst of the interconnected processes of learning and development. Higher education professionals should be mindful of how they are perceived, should never belittle or demean students, and should consider how student political engagement might complement both student learning and institutional missions. To put it simply, if institutions of higher education are intended to create opportunities for social mobility and to foster a critical and engaged citizenry, it follows logically that the same institutions should expect to see student political engagement on their campuses.

While understanding these issues conceptually and in context is critical, they can lead to awkward or uncomfortable conversations. As students are learning more about their own identities and learning how to engage their agency and their voice, those who work in higher education are frequently confronted with these kinds of conversations. When this happens administrators would do well to choose to listen first. Understanding that you've been heard can be a powerful beginning to a conversation, even if that conversation ultimately becomes a negotiation. While true, administrators should be prepared for the reality that simply hearing or having a dialogue with students is not enough. We have to be willing to evolve our campus practices, structures, and processes to meet students' evolving needs. Doing this work effectively looks like intentionally moving beyond outdated positional paradigms of power and acknowledging that institutions and their cultures are created and reproduced by all stakeholder groups.

In recent years, tensions have frequently reached pique around invited speakers on some campuses. The right for a student group to invite a speaker to their campus, or for faculty or administrators to do so, relies on an interconnected series of legal issues and institutional policies. The legal issues, particularly around First Amendment speech, are different depending on whether an institution is public or private. On the other hand, institutions have much greater control over how they structure their own policies and procedures. While colleges and universities should take care not to create policies that are narrowly targeted or constitute viewpoint discrimination, it has also become clear in recent years that institutions typically do not have a regular review process in place once a policy is established.

Admittedly, this is not one of the most attractive areas of work in higher education administration. However, a policy about inviting speakers to campus, time/place/manner restrictions on campus speech, and the like may have been written years or even decades ago and may result in unintended consequences for campuses. Moreover, creating or amending policies in the aftermath of a major campus incident could also lead to policies that are overly restrictive or untenable in the long term. Regular review of all policies should be enacted on campuses and key leaders should be held accountable for the process.

Perception, both on and off campus, also becomes magnified during incidents involving invited speakers. Protests can make national headlines, social media can amplify voices almost instantaneously, and administrators can appear sluggish in their responses. As a result, each campus should undertake the work to develop, game out, and keep updated plans for such situations. Though perhaps not widely known, this sort of preparation for emergency management on campus has become increasingly commonplace, and administrators have a responsibility to create the time and space to do this planning before a major incident erupts on campus.

Safe Spaces and Trigger Warnings

The popular media has both increased awareness of and excoriated the concepts of safe spaces and trigger warnings in higher education. The most common critiques seem to rely on the notion that these practices constitute coddling students, are not available in "real life" or employment contexts, or are part of some larger nefarious agenda. In practice, safe spaces and trigger warnings have evolved as tools that may be useful to some populations or when addressing certain topics.

A root concern here is the notion that higher education ought to prepare students for post-graduation employment by making the higher education experience closely resemble an employment context. This is a neoliberal construct that présumés that work, and in particular efficient work, is prized above all else and is contrary to the mission and values of many colleges and universities.

Improved employment opportunities is and should be one benefit of postsecondary study. Better employment opportunities and lifetime earnings are not achieved by college graduates simply because they learned concrete skills in higher education. The notion should be dismissed as foolishly simple on its very face when one considers that students spend two or four years earning a credential and then, minimally in most cases, four decades at work.

Establishing a safe space for certain groups is derived from a recognition that experiences in higher education vary, at least in part, based on an individual's identities. The cognitive and developmental work that happens when higher education functions well are not easy, direct, or linear experiences. This work is recursive and is always happening in a larger societal context where issues of power, oppression, and marginalization are not suspended.

Trigger warnings have received particular attention in recent years and are sometimes parodied without even a basic understanding of what they are and why they might exist. Even a glancing understanding of trauma as modern psychological and medical professionals understand it makes it clear that trauma has real, physiological, and lasting impacts on humans. Higher education is supposed to be a space where everyone admitted to study has the opportunity to learn, and providing a small warning to those who have experienced trauma that a discussion about trauma is beginning is not unreasonable. To the critics who lob cheap non sequiturs such as, "there are no trigger warnings at my job," we might ask, "does your job regularly require you to discuss or consider human trauma like abuse, sexual violence, childhood sexual assault, and the like?"

In essence, supposed concerns over such tools is often no more than political theater from those who would use social identities and experiences with trauma as wedge issues. Once we understand the influence of neoliberal tendencies in higher education, the history and evolution of students and their needs, and the broader mission of most institutions, the inanity of such critiques is laid bare. Higher education is not job training, students and their needs are changing, and higher education owes its students a duty to understand these changes to try to respond to and support them with new tools.

Political Engagement For and By Whom?

As students have re-engaged in political discourse and activism in recent years, higher education administrators have tended to focus on the logistics and legalities of managing what this means to an institution, its reputation, town-gown relations, donors, and alumni. In other words, energy and focus have been largely lower order concerns. Impacts of student activism on these groups does matter but taking such a management approach singularly misses the mark.

Students engaging in political processes and activism are engaging in and applying learning in myriad ways. Coupled with the elementary precept that interest enhances learning, this means administrators have a powerful opportunity to engage students intellectually around these issues when framed as an opportunity for student learning. When considered this way, we might ask different questions about student political engagement. For example, who on campus is actually taking up this work? Is it rooted in a campus incident or something broader? Is it about identity, economics, structures, or other societal issues?

Politicization of Education on Human Dignity and Student Consumerism

The increased politicization of higher education over the last decade has been particularly palpable when it comes to understanding student political engagement and activism. While there is no shortage of evidence that higher education faculty and leaders are disproportionately likely to identify as liberal or progressive, the notion that colleges and universities are in effect indoctrinating undergraduate students with a radical political agenda has no merit. This rhetoric is a consequence of scapegoating higher education for continually evolving social and cultural norms.

That said, when such rhetoric is coupled with the concerns above regarding institutional image and perception, it can have an impact on administrative decision making. If we take a philosophical understanding of higher education as job training, then an institution fostering or supporting student political engagement might seem strange. However, if the approach to education is rooted in developing a critical and engaged citizenry, as most mission statements suggest, it follows that students need to consider ideas beyond the borders of their disciplines, campuses, and intended professions.

Institutions often couch this kind of student engagement in the discourse of human dignity, social justice, or equity. The caustic and highly polarized political rhetoric around this kind of a liberal education uses terms like the "politicization of higher education." As higher education scholar D-L Stewart (2018) recently asserted, "educating people about respect for human dignity is not owned by any political or social ideology" (p. 1). Stewart also acknowledges that the history of higher education is one rooted in oppression and marginalization, meaning that higher education today has a responsibility to educate students and stakeholders about the ongoing ripple effects of these practices. In essence, succumbing to the notion that an education that includes examining human dignity and social justice is a political exercise serves as a chilling effect to student political engagement and to the realization of most institutional missions.

Developing a deeper understanding of the interplay between institutions and students around political engagement also affects how we make sense of overall student-institution relations. Beginning in the 1990s, researchers began documenting notions of student consumerism, wherein both students and institutions may conceptualize students as customers and institutions as businesses. The simplistic, transactional understanding of education has certainly been exacerbated by the ongoing neoliberalization of higher education, and it begins to fall apart when we consider the responsibility an institution might have to support students in social and political engagement.

Indeed, if the role of higher education writ large is about more than job training, and student learning and development can be served in part by student social and political engagement, then it seems clear that American higher education is a public good. This notion meshes with funding models and public opinion from earlier in the twentieth century but is implicitly rejected by political rhetoric today.

In more practical terms, higher education professionals and administrators face a substantive challenge in determining both how their support of or reaction to these kinds of student engagement intersects with their mission and how to help their stakeholders understand the importance of this work. Those working in such roles should have regular, proactive conversations on their campuses about how to respond to student social and political engagement, and these conversations may include students themselves. In addition, effective higher education leaders will also have proactive conversations with their stakeholders about this kind of student engagement, how the institution mission and values will inform the ways administrators interact with students in these spaces, and how such engagement is a net positive for the institution. This work requires careful planning and a firm understanding of the political realities for a college or university, but it can lead to positive outcomes for all involved.

Ponder

What is the tone and tenor of student social and political engagement on your campus, both among students and faculty/staff?

What policies around such engagement are in place and when were they last reviewed?

How do you support staff and faculty in creating safe spaces and trigger warnings? How have you responded to critiques from other constituent groups?

How might your institution prepare to respond to critics who say you are brainwashing the youth of our country?

_____
_____
_____
_____
_____
_____
_____
_____
_____

References

Stewart, D.-L. (2018). Refuting the politicization of student affairs work. *Inside Higher Ed.* Retrieved from https://www.insidehighered.com/views/2018/11/08/student-affairs-administrators-arent-socializing-students-leftist-ideology-opinion

Section III
Teaching and Learning

By Adam Elias

Teaching and Learning

Course Delivery

This section of the book examines trends in teaching and learning. This will not involve microscopic views of specific pedagogies, but larger emergent variables that have deeply affected the practice of teaching in higher education within the last two decades, and most specifically within the past several years. These chapters will look at high-level concepts with broad application, though the implications of each can vary dramatically among institutions and classrooms. Appropriately, we begin with the very concept of educational delivery.

If higher education institutions deliver a service, or a product, what is it? Some would say it's knowledge, others might suggest experience. It's not difficult to argue that the service provided is a synthesis of the two—an educational experience. Such a product is typically packaged in degrees, made up of something we have come to call *the course*. Measured in credits and weighed in seat time, for over the past century, the course has been the standard method by which institutions deliver their product to students, and when someone referred to a college class, one generally knew what to expect. Then, one day, the Internet came along. If anything has earned the title of "disruptor" in twenty-first century higher education, that notoriety belongs to the World Wide Web.

The Internet as the Great Disruptor

One cannot talk in depth about teaching and learning trends without first touching upon the relatively recent technological shifts that continue to affect the entire industry daily. As we begin the section of this book reflecting on trends in course delivery, it's critical to set the context: our world continues to reinvent itself regularly, via technology. Change is the constant, and now it moves at high speeds.

The Internet has changed every aspect of human life. Even in the mid-1980s, the potential for computer networks to revolutionize communication was starting to become apparent; Ithiel de la Sola Pool (1984) identified computer communication as "one of the four most fundamental changes in the history of communications technology," alongside writing, the printing press, and telegraphy. Now, the Internet has been around for so long that it can be difficult to remember the last time we engaged in the manual predecessors of daily tasks that are now conducted primarily through gadgets and information superhighways; the old dirt roads of yesteryear are long overgrown. From communication to calculation to capitalistic consumption, everything happens so frequently through a connected device. Some would say this has advanced life tremendously; others would describe this as a slow crawl to ruin. Either way, our little blue globe has been forever altered.

And we're not even talking about teaching yet.

In the midst of this change, the practice of teaching has been completely and utterly upended. Since the phrase "disruptive innovation" was coined by Harvard Business School professors Joseph Bower and Clayton Christensen in *Harvard Business Review* in 1995, the word "disruption" has been a staple, if not overused, component of any self-respecting futurists' lexicon. When the Internet truly went mainstream in the early 1990s, it did not take long for a great many higher education stakeholders to connect the dial-up dots and identify the impending doom of their livelihood, superseded by an inferior type of impersonal education that occurred through online delivery. Mind you, at the same time began whispers of a similar fate for the United States Postal Service, as the American people would one day turn their back on paper mail altogether, in light of their newfound ability to send mail electronically.

At least in the public conversation that ensued, the middleground was often completely overlooked, and the "for/against" narrative that arose presented a false dilemma to faculty and higher education administrators everywhere, coloring the way forward in unpleasant shades that implied a coming extinction of traditional course deliveries and modalities. According to Harasim (2000), "while developments in the 1980s and 1990s prepared for a revolution in the field of education, most of the noise generated in the media questioned the value and quality of online education and expressed the concerns of some faculty who felt they would be displaced by less well-trained staff" (p.42). People flipped out, and for good reason; were colleges and universities on their death beds, laid low by modems and mice?

That doomsday has not yet come to pass, and though the hallowed halls of higher education institutions are only slightly scarcer than they were in the mid-90's (though easier to find, thanks to Google Maps), they're undoubtedly different. Much of the disruption that occurred from the rise of online teaching was based on fear, and was perhaps unfounded. Yes, more than two decades into the introduction of online classes, lo and behold, brick-and-mortar campuses are still all around us. Yet, over that same time, hundreds, if not thousands, of faculty have come to near blows in arguing for their institutions to either ride the winds of change to new heights, or dig in and wait for the storm to pass.

When online delivery started to seem a viable modality for colleges and universities, early adopters sprinted toward it. However, those early efforts largely focused on replicating existing teaching methodologies at a distance, rather than inventing new pedagogies altogether. As a result, online delivery became the latest iteration of distance learning—shifting from a reliance on postal service to dial-up service. The stigma long associated with correspondence courses soon characterized online delivery, too, and with it came the questioning of its effectiveness. Yet, "these early offerings did provide rapid and valuable lessons into what constitutes effective learning in this new mode of education delivery" (Siemens, Gašević, & Dawson, 2015, p.96). Following more than three decades of development, taking place alongside technological leaps and bounds that vastly expanded wireless connections while simultaneously shrinking devices, online educational delivery has transcended trend status, and flourished into a paradigm shift.

Blended Delivery

As traditional teaching methods and delivery models evolved in response to the Internet, all manners of experimentation were afoot. Globally, teachers began to test new tools and pedagogies, often from the comfort of a traditional classroom. From these "dual roots" (Siemens, Gasevic, & Dawson, 2015, p.65) was born what we now call blended teaching—an irregular and undefined assortment of traditional site-based instruction with web-based technologies and resources. Somewhat ironically, it is in blended teaching, between traditional and completely online delivery, where some of the most exciting innovation has arisen in recent years.

Defining blended teaching can be a very high-level taxonomy, covering a multitude of strategies and techniques, some feeling much trendier than others. The common thread is an online component, though its size and significance can vary substantially. Concordia University-Portland (2013) breaks down blended learning into four different models, based on how a student moves between site-based learning and online learning: rotation (schedule set by instructor), flex (online unless student chooses site-based support), enhanced virtual (some pre-set site-based time, the rest online), and self-blend (completely self-paced, individually customized around a particular student). These categories closely resemble similar labels developed by Horn and Staker (Christensen Institute, 2019). Within these four categories reside a near endless combination of approaches to teaching, whether reliant on distance, or despite it.

The beauty of blended delivery in modern classrooms is the ability for faculty to utilize the best of both traditional and digital pedagogies. Granted, this is old news. What is the basis for its inclusion in a book on trends?

The latest iteration in blended delivery is all about choice, and not just on the faculty side of the table. Rather than setting clear parameters around how a course is delivered, institutions are increasingly opening all channels of engagement to students. It's an ambitious approach that maximizes the learner's control over how they will participate in a class, whether by attending on-site meetings, consuming online materials, joining classmates via web-conferencing, or any other now-typical form of student engagement. Often, colleges already offer all of these opportunities (meeting face-to-face or online) and materials (print or online), and this sort of "omni-modality" is merely synthesizing and coordinating the availability of all of those options in a single course context.

Make no mistake, this delivery model is rife with challenges for institutions; in an era where students know full well that they have options, they're going to choose how they engage, and so institutions have to meet students on *their* terms. Though it has been common practice for a long time, attempting to restrict student choice of format is a risky game for institutions to play in today's market. Instead, Selingo (2018) argues that student preferences should be embraced, and institutional strategies diversified in order to become more truly learner-centered.

The kicker here is that prepping such a heavily blended course is more complicated—there is no real shortcut to creating an experience across multiple modalities, without doing the work that would normally be required for each. But once that work is done, institutions can enjoy plenty of benefits, including reaching expanded populations while maintaining a high degree of efficiency. The possibilities are wide open, and institutions gain a great amount of flexibility through the philosophy that a course is a course is a course, for any student needs or preferences. Rather than offering several sections of a class, all based on a singular modality, a single section/instance of a class can be offered, and opened to students, wherever they are, or want to be.

While this model is not yet widespread, at least with any consistency, a number of institutions are beginning to experiment with deconstructing the traditional parameters around course delivery, including the University of Central Florida (EAB, 2017). The University of Texas at Austin has often been highlighted for its introductory psychology course delivered in a format akin to a talk show, with two faculty leading the discussion in front of a studio audience, complete with the studio-level production facilities and equipment you'd expect at your local news station's headquarters (Blumenstyk, 2016). Students can choose to occupy a seat in the studio, but the rest—around 1,500 a semester—engage at a distance, both synchronously (think your favorite weekly TV show) and asynchronously, through a variety of online channels and media.

While it is common practice for institutions to allow students to navigate from online classes to site-based classes over the course of their program, further blending those lines can be a complex logistical effort. Yet, the opportunities for faculty creativity in new blended models of course delivery are immense. Indeed, the state of the higher education market demands this kind of innovation.

The Future of Education Delivery

While studies continue to roll in suggesting a crisis in the public's perceived value of a college degree, droves of traditional students aren't going to begin abandoning the opportunities college provides to leave their parents' homes. Yet, to remain viable, institutions are going to have to court a far wider variety of students; Selingo (2018) refers to this challenge as the need for "segmentation" in the ways colleges and universities frame themselves as providers of academic experiences—becoming what target populations want and need, even if the result is a seemingly-fragmented institution, with multiple personalities. While this philosophy is often operationalized in student affairs and services, it must also be considered in the context of course delivery.

Digital formats of course delivery will continue to play a critical role in higher ed, and institutions must be prepared to better mold, shape, and blend their delivery models to those that suit student needs, as well as preferences. This isn't about becoming all things to all people, but becoming the *right* thing for the *sought* people. Thus, blended delivery—while born of online teaching—is set to evolve from its parentage, from a term describing a specific approach to teaching that is half-tangible/half-virtual, to a broader kind of institutional philosophy that customizes the delivery of an academic experience to a program's students. As web-based channels of interaction continue to become just another aspect of the postsecondary landscape, the technology of these pathways will be less a defining characteristic, and more an essential aspect of infrastructure. The talk will no longer be about online teaching, or even blended teaching; it will all just be teaching.

Ponder

What fears keep your institution from engaging in new delivery models?

_____
_____
_____
_____
_____
_____
_____
_____

Are new delivery models being sought for the right reasons? Is your institution's mission behind the search/attempt?

_____
_____
_____
_____
_____
_____
_____

Is your institution still engaged in the on-site versus online argument? If so, have the loudest on each side been engaged in cooperative opportunities? Have any faculty co-taught in a mixed-mode class?

How are faculty at your institution engaging in blended teaching?

What is your institution's plan for maintaining its identity amidst the ebb and flow of differing delivery models?

References

Blumenstyk, G. (2016). Same time, many locations: Online education goes back to its origins. *The Chronicle of Higher Education.* Retrieved from https://www.chronicle.com/article/Same-Time-Many-Locations-/236788?CID=relearning&elqTrackId=7b7c29bebfff4bb691b420be0307e21d&elq=ad1aaf3d1fe845b3910a17ef2a82fe82&elqaid=20987&elqat=1&elqCampaignId=9946.

Bower, J. L., & Christensen, C. M. (1995). Disruptive technologies: Catching the wave. *Harvard Business Review* (January-February), 43-53.

Christensen Institute. (2019). *Blended learning definitions.* Retrieved from https://www.christenseninstitute.org/blended-learning-definitions-and-models/

Concordia University. (2013). Four blended teaching models. Retrieved from https://education.cu-portland.edu/blog/classroom-resources/four-blended-learning-models/

de la Sola Pool, I. (1984). Communications flows: A census in the United States and Japan. Amsterdam: University of Tokyo Press.

EAB. (2017). Why would an on-campus student take online classes? *EAB Daily Briefing* (March 27, 2017). Retrieved from https://www.eab.com/daily-briefing/2017/03/27/why-would-an-on-campus-student-take-online-classes

Harasim, L. (2000). Shift happens: Online education as a new paradigm in learning. *The Internet and Higher Education, 3*(1-2), 41-61.

Harris, J. (2002). "Brief History of American Academic Credit System: A Recipe for Incoherence in Student Learning" (PDF). Samford University. Archived from the original (PDF) on December 20, 2005. Retrieved June 20, 2006.

Selingo, J.J. (2018). *The Future Learners.* Pearson.

Siemens, G., Gašević, D., & Dawson, S. (2015). Preparing for the digital university: A review of the history and current state of distance, blended, and online learning.

Teaching and Learning

Learning Environments

Learning environments in higher education have long been defined rather simply and narrowly: four walls with a roof, desks, chairs, and maybe some kind of canvas or stage for the instructor. If one were to ask a stranger where students learn, nine times out of ten, the response would be, "A classroom." Until the last several decades, in educational contexts, teaching and learning have been contained within the same place; encoding and decoding knowledge occurred over short physical distances, often no more than a few feet away.

Learning environments aren't what they used to be, but this topic has been a site of innovation long before the virtual asphalt was poured for the information superhighway. Educators have long understood that both teaching and learning can take place anywhere. Remember Plato and Aristotle as portrayed in Raphael's famous fresco, "The School of Athens?" They were on a walk. While few dispute that learning can happen anywhere, in a structured sense, that sentiment hasn't gained much traction until recently. And, despite the persistence of the traditional classroom, it is not difficult to find a wide variety of learning environments in use by postsecondary institutions. How those spaces are being used accounts for some of the most fascinating recent trends in higher education.

Classrooms

Postsecondary educators continue to hold a special place in their hearts for the traditional classroom, and for good reason. Despite the meteoric rise of online learning at the end of the twentieth century, physical classrooms continue to be a constant in the higher education landscape. While many of these look eerily similar to how they did a hundred years ago, others have benefited from a literal new coat of paint, new kinds of furniture and trimmings, and other bells and whistles. The classroom furniture industry is shockingly lucrative.

Many such updates to the traditional classroom have been fueled by the trend of active learning, which seeks to reinvent the passive didactic experience of the traditional classroom by introducing activities centered on movement and social interaction. The research behind this approach indicates that involving students in a more active way promotes a deeper understanding of the subject matter, and institutions have plunged head first into initiatives to retool physical classrooms to support and promote active learning, to the joyful boon of classroom furniture vendors worldwide. Often, these environments end up being colorful, capable, and coveted by those scheduled to teach in the old rooms.

Yet, whatever they are called, and whatever they contain, such physical spaces continue to serve as the bedrock of the traditional classroom-based approach to educational delivery. As long as students remain social creatures, the traditional classroom will have a place on college campuses. Even so, faculty—and particularly those who have been at the same institution for a long while—can sometimes turn a blind eye to their regular teaching spaces, focusing more on content that context. While discussions about the condition and appeal of physical classrooms can seem superfluous in times of budget crunches, the environment can be an important variable in student learning. The emergent trend of active learning provides faculty and administrators with a wealth of research and resources to make new cases for improving classrooms, particularly if active learning is incorporated into the proposal.

Community-Based Learning

The physical classroom isn't the only traditional learning environment of higher education that continues to serve as a site of teaching and learning trends. In fact, what is *beyond* the four walls has seen a resurgence in importance for institutions seeking to establish themselves as unique in a crowded market, and as relevant to a generation acutely focused on ideas of connection, community engagement, or social justice.

While the Information Age has connected people in extraordinary ways, and has led to sweeping expansions in access to postsecondary education online, a common question centers on what is lost in that digitally-induced landscape. It's a critical question. Some studies suggest that millennial students are, despite their wireless connectivity, strikingly disconnected from their peers, and less able to cope with stressors that prior generations easily managed (Twenge, 2017). It's easy to blame devices and the distances they create. All the while, students across the United States continue to question the value of a college education. Building and strengthening community bonds has emerged as a potential opportunity for higher ed institutions to have a more intrusive positive impact on their students, while also making a stronger case for their value.

Thus, institutions are doubling-down on the tangible experience of learning within a community-centered context. Community-based learning, like blended teaching, serves as an umbrella term for a multitude of approaches to instruction; this involves creating a community context for learning, and engaging students in projects, environments, and encounters that yield learning outcomes in socially constructive ways. CBL is a form of experiential learning, standing alongside such staples as the internship, co-op, field experience, and others. Experiential learning is certainly not a new concept, but institutions are more frequently using community-based learning to provide students with an effective and memorable experience that also benefits the actual neighborhoods and cities in which they exist. While the approach has more than its fair share of detractors who consider it little more than a gimmick or PR strategy without substantial educational benefits, the effectiveness of such an approach lies in the prep work of the instructor, the legitimate connections between activities and learning outcomes, and the ability to assess and evaluate the experience. The sky is the limit in how such an approach to teaching is implemented, and certainly, faculty were teaching in this way long before the phrase "community-based learning" was coined. Even so, at a higher institutional level, this pedagogical approach carries immense possibilities for colleges and universities that seek to differentiate themselves from the pack.

Perhaps more importantly, institutions can no longer afford to separate themselves from the local community; indeed, effective and successful institutions must recognize their community relationships as symbiotic, elevating the importance of the potential for learning they hold. By fostering these relationships, institutions, communities, and the stakeholders in both can enjoy significant benefits beyond attracting change-agent students, including progress toward some of the loftier philosophical goals embedded in the institution's mission.

The possibilities of community-based learning arrangements are endless when community organizations and actors are willing to be part of the equation. A single community partner, such as a nonprofit organization, can provide opportunities for engagement across a number of subject areas and specialties. Think of a local homeless shelter and the opportunities for students in majors such as psychology, nursing, public health, sociology, physical therapy, and others. Management students could analyze a particular problem of the organization for a senior seminar. Communication students could gain firsthand experience by running the organization's PR campaign. Students in health care programs can gain an understanding of services provided by a public health organization and how they affect the welfare of the region, while even coordinating clinics. With the right care to ensure that learning objectives are front-and-center, such intersection between the institution and the community can be mutually beneficial, and provide real-world experience that students may lack upon degree completion.

What's more, community-based learning environments also speak volumes to a generation as interested as ever in making a difference in their communities, and for those for whom that isn't a priority, it can even change attitudes toward civic engagement—a challenging goal that is often embedded in institutional missions in some way. In short, it's not difficult to reach consensus that an institution's place in its community is critical, and can serve as a valuable source of learning through creative and innovative partnerships.

Learning Management Systems

Certainly, it is not necessary to cross the digital divide to find nontraditional learning environments, but anyone with an ear to the ground would be lax *not* to spend time on the ways teaching and learning occur in digital spaces. The first of this kind has risen to prominence, to the point that nearly every higher education institution in the nation has one: learning management systems (LMS). The nomenclature has varied over the last two decades; these are sometimes called "course management systems," but the variety of uses they serve in both the public and private sectors has led to a general zeroing in on using the term "learning" rather than "course." As more innovative approaches are attempted in the digital space, such terminology allows a more general application.

According to Pomerantz, Brown, and Brooks (2018), the LMS has become critical to teaching and learning. Almost every higher education institution deploys at least one if not multiple LMS platforms. Indeed, the rate of LMS adoption by institutions (99%) and by faculty (88%) puts it in the category with cars and cellphones as among the most widely adopted technologies in the United States. Despite this ubiquity, a definition is still important. An institution's learning management system is its digital and cloud-based application for academic use, most commonly involving discrete web spaces for classes or course sections. In essence, the LMS can be understood as the virtual schoolhouse, with virtual classrooms inside. Just as institutions require personnel to maintain physical campuses and facilities, so too are such virtual environments in need of a variety of groundskeepers to keep them functional and aesthetically appropriate. In contrast to physical campus spaces, in which most users understand how to navigate halls, write on whiteboards, and open the right doors, the LMS carries with it an added need for personnel to provide training for potential users. To date, most institutions that utilize an LMS also dedicate staff to that purpose. Thus, a kind of meta-learning often occurs in the lead-up to utilizing an LMS for academic delivery.

For the most part, learning management systems all do the same thing. Finding the right fit is often more about cost and alignment with institutional resources than it is about the best product. Large institutions or systems may opt for a costly product that is hosted centrally, off-site. Smaller institutions may prefer to host their own platform, such as Moodle, in-house. Regardless of the choice made, faculty support of the LMS is critical; they must be involved in decisions that affect teaching, receive professional development, and have access to just-in-time support for a variety of challenges and issues that are sure to arise in the process of actually teaching.

The LMS industry has grown to a startling size, and this is a topic on which a particular industry's market trends has direct implications for teaching. When an institution selects or changes its LMS, virtually every single student at the institution is affected. As the competition has quickened its pace over the last decade, the fallout has affected far more students than any simple classroom renovation ever could.

The biggest name in this space has long been Blackboard, though that reign appears to be nearing its end as that platform continues to lose its market dominance to other rising stars. Instructure's Canvas has gained tremendous momentum, to the point that it may soon overtake Blackboard's crown for being the official LMS for most US institutions (Hill, 2017). Indeed, as of the time of this writing, the two are neck-and-neck, with the trend line suggesting that Canvas will have the upper-hand by 2021; this will be a true milestone in the saga of online learning. The open-source behemoth, Moodle, has maintained its top-three standing, secure in its role as the chosen LMS for institutions seeking to wield greater control of their own technologies. This showing is supported by the fact that as more institutions utilize Moodle for longer periods of time, the number of useful add-ins, visual designs and themes, and sources for crowd-sourcing troubleshooting increases as well.

The topic of digital learning environments opens an intriguing Pandora's Box for higher education institutions. Few LMS products allow those institutions to host the product on their own campus premises, with the exception of the open-source Moodle. As the software market has shifted to software-as-a-service (SAAS) model, so, too, has the LMS market. Institutions now pay hefty fees, often per student, to have stable access to an LMS, though the vast majority of the operation is managed by the product's owner, at a data center somewhere else in the United States. Because the LMS is so pervasive in higher education, colleges and universities are finding themselves in a state of indentured servitude to LMS corporations, feeling as though there are few alternatives to shelling out hundreds of thousands of dollars in some cases. Institutions that self-host their own LMS must dedicate sufficient resources—both technical as well as personnel—to ensure their product is secure, up-to-date, and functional.

That may be a welcome trade-off, considering the vast savings. Yet, since SAAS LMS solutions have come so far, institutional decision-makers may be enticed by the bells and whistles of near-endless lists of features that the vendor would provide and manage. The expanded efficiency and capabilities can be a real draw, but so can the ability to maintain control of the institution's own tools, including upgrade timelines and customization. While vendors often provide flexibility in some of these areas, at the end of the day, institutions are paying for access to a product that they do not own.

As open-source options shrink and the LMS market continues to expand, learning environments will continue to be one of the most significant sites of innovation in teaching over the next several years. While the LMS as a concept is nothing new, this landscape is absolutely being reinvented continually.

Ponder

Does your institution have a process in place to tie expenditures on learning environments (traditional or nontraditional) to learning benefits? What would such a process look like?

Does your institution include a representative body of stakeholders who regularly evaluate learning environments, both physical and digital?

If your institution does not centrally coordinate community-based learning initiatives, what might such an endeavor look like?

How are community-based learning initiatives evaluated to ensure comparability with—or superiority over—other kinds of learning environments?

Has your institution honestly discussed both the benefits and risks involved in LMS options? Do sufficient resources exist to consider an open-source option?

References

Hill, P. (2017) *State of higher ed LMS market for US and Canada: Fall 2017 edition.* eLiterate. Retrieved from https://eliterate.us/state-higher-ed-lms-market-us-canada-fall-2017-edition/

Pomerantz, J., Brown, M., & Brooks, D.C. (2018). *Foundations for a next generation digital learning environment: Faculty, students, and the LMS.* Research report. Louisville, CO: ECAR.

Twenge, J.M. (2017) *Have smartphones destroyed a generation?* The Atlantic. Retrieved from https://www.theatlantic.com/magazine/archive/2017/09/has-the-smartphone-destroyed-a-generation/534198/

Teaching and Learning
Media Platforms

As discussed in the previous chapter, when visualizing the concept of teaching, the didactic default reigns supreme; the most common imagery is still a classroom setting, with the teacher at the front, capturing the attention of students with all the gusto of Robin Williams' John Keating in *Dead Poets Society*. While the modern reality is becoming further removed from this ideal every year, this representation has been characteristic of higher education for a long time. At least in the tradition of Western civilization, information has been orally delivered by a teacher, in a very direct sense. Yet, as the nature and environments of that delivery shifts, so too must the medium of instruction.

While media has never been more pervasive or conspicuous than it is in the Digital Age, by no means is it novel. When the printing press began to bring the written word to the masses in the fifteenth century, the common folk gained a great victory in the ability to self-teach. Particularly during the Enlightenment of the eighteenth century, the mass production of popular and classic works threw open the door for individuals to learn in ways that were not centrally dependent on another living, breathing human being.

In this sense, though it was a slow start, the rise of the printing press forced the evolution of higher education, as students began to reference primary sources. Teachers began to change from sources of truth to conveyers of knowledge, packaging and presenting subject matter into messages that were palatable and appropriate to their students. This was the dominant approach in the twentieth century, as students consumed standardized information on their own—i.e., read the course text—and then spent classroom time reviewing, discussing, or otherwise engaging with the subject matter under the direct guidance of the professor. With variation, this model has persisted.

In this paradigm, the act of teaching and the learning materials that support that act enjoy a kind of symbiotic relationship. One would be hard-pressed to find a self-respecting professor with little regard for her textbook; the materials represent instructor choice, and serve as an extension of the teacher. Textbook publishers rely on teachers to adopt their textbooks, historically guaranteeing that classrooms full of students purchase those books (from the student perspective, this might be better characterized as a parasitic relationship). Regardless, for better or worse, somewhere along the trail of change, the classroom experience and class materials became two sides of the same coin. The very idea of a class without hard-bound textbooks or other expensive course materials became a scarlet letter of questionable quality.

Modern Materials

That is all changing, though perhaps not in the way that many have hoped. The technological changes of the last two decades have utterly transformed print media, and this includes textbook publishers. As online materials, and specifically eBooks, began to become more common, doubt was cast on the long-term viability of the print market, and indeed, many publishers have since shuttered, unable to adapt to a market dominated by Amazon, a retailer of both print and emergent electronic formats. Similarly, academic publishers saw their lives flash before their eyes in the early 2000s, but due in no small part to the means they had accumulated through the business model that had essentially locked in sales on a semesterly basis, the largest of these entities were able to adapt. Though the same cannot be said for many universities' in-house publishers. This existential threat to Big Textbook resulted in a transformation more akin to the status of the software industry than the book market.

And so, when speaking of course materials today, increasingly, we are actually speaking more of digital media platforms than textbooks, with far more interactivity. All of the biggest names in academic textbook publishing have strode into this arena: Pearson, McGraw-Hill, Cengage, and the rest. These materials often include a traditional academic text in electronic form—an eBook version of a textbook. Yet, these platforms are typically just the lowest rung of a ladder of digital materials, serving as a basis for more advanced features, like one might expect to encounter when buying a new car; the basic model is only the starting point. How elaborate would you like your experience to be?

Beyond the basic course text, academic media platforms now include curated video, galleries of pertinent images, presentations that are both animated and interactive, and most recently, activities and pathways that are adaptive, adjusting a student's experience based on how well that student demonstrates understanding. Yes, artificial intelligence is blossoming in the world of digital academic media, providing students with a level of class customization far beyond what faculty could hope to offer in traditional classes.

As easy as it is to roll one's eyes at the complex offerings a simple textbook may now afford, this brave new world in academic materials may actually be worth something, or at the very least, it may be an effective way of engaging the modern student. For all their pomp and spectacle, digital media platforms provide many benefits beyond their print predecessors, including portability, accessibility, and variety, to name a few.

Benefits

Three decades ago, arriving at your beachfront rental, only to realize your favorite book—or your needed textbook—was left on your bedside table at home meant one of two things: a replacement would have to be sought in a local bookshop, or you'd have to go without it. Today's media platforms pose no such risk. Even if one's eBook reader is inadvertently left behind, the majority of publishers and electronic media ecosystems allow cloud-based access from a variety of devices. While it may mean less comfortable reading time than a Kindle would provide, a laptop would still provide access through cloud technologies. Our media now follows us, wherever we may go.

Digital media platforms also provide a level of accessibility, particularly for those with disabilities, that was never possible with print materials. Screen-reading technology has advanced by leaps and bounds, providing instant access to content for those with visual impairments. Prior to that development, countless students relied upon either braille texts or another living, breathing human to read for them. For digital video materials, captions are increasingly becoming a standard feature, having received numerous newsworthy boosts from judicial precedent, federal mandates, and, perhaps ironically, the competition fueled by a capitalist economy which only began to pursue accommodations when it became profitable

The shift in academic media platforms, from print textbooks to digital materials, serves another purpose, which may be most critical of all: more fluently speaking the language of student engagement. In the age of print textbooks, the production team of such materials often included only the textbook author—an academic—and that person's editor and publisher. Sure, a number of other readers and key players shared roles, such as sprucing up the text with images and charts. However, in the era of digital platforms for academic materials, entire teams of private sector software developers—often with limited background in a given discipline—are involved in producing a robust package of digital content, based around a traditional text, with a sole purpose: to engage the student, capture interest, and produce results. Publishers are well aware of the rising importance of data in higher education, and recognize that student success is among the most critical metrics in gauging the effectiveness of a course, and by extension, the instructor. When materials promote success, everyone wins: students pass, instructors demonstrate skill in their craft, and institutions gather evidence of effectiveness of their choices.

As digital media platforms become more complex and occupy more significant roles in both conveying content and engaging students in a course—both roles that instructors have historically occupied—their ability to move the ball and produce results can cause seismic shifts in academic circles. Now more than ever, publishers have a vested interest in students actually doing well in courses using their platforms. Intuitively, if a student enjoys engaging with academic media, they are more likely to use it more consistently, and its positive effects on the learning process can be more evident.

A New Frontier in eCommerce

For all the promise of digital media platforms in postsecondary education, this topic is not without a dark side. Not long ago, an expensive textbook could be perceived as a justifiable purchase in part due to its utility in a professional setting after a student graduates. Or, it could simply be sold back to the bookstore at semester's end. These days, though, publishers are shifting not just to an eBook model, but one most accurately described as "software-as-a-service," or SAAS. *"Enjoyed the interactive materials you used in class? It's yours—for a low fee of $150 per semester for the rest of your life."* To be fair, this trend of deconstructing student ownership of materials under the guise of low cost has been going on in the college bookstore world for many years now, under the practice of textbook rentals. Counter-intuitively, though, one might find a kind of ironic value in this. As a growing subset of American culture seeks greater simplicity through the divestment of excessive physical possessions, the idea of bookshelves loaded with aging college textbooks may not as appealing as it once was. Still, the expense remains, and may be perceived as disproportionate to the role the materials play in learning.

While many institutions consider digital literacy, it is very clear that during students' time in college—and more and more, even before they arrive—they become experts in media consumption, regardless of institutional strategy. Students have a trove of experience in this area, whether it's consuming movies, TV, or music, navigating the Internet, downloading and using apps, etc., and it's not difficult to see through the need to pay a steep sticker price for something only needed sparingly or temporarily. This is not an assumed need to today's students, and some may simply forgo the purchase altogether, and face the consequences.

Open Education Resources

Earlier, it was suggested that the transformation of media platforms in the context of course materials was not the revolution for which many had hoped. It certainly sounds very exciting, and a number of benefits have been identified. Even so, as the possibilities of modern media have developed since the turn of the century, no small number of educators have hoped and advocated for a substantial rise in the adoption of open education resources, or OER. This argument centers on the fact that information is more widely and freely available than it ever has been. So, why must students still be saddled with the responsibility of paying for expensive course materials—flashy and interactive as they may be—behind publisher paywalls? Could not students learn just as much, if not more, from openly-accessible materials all over the web?

This is an important question that has unfortunately gained far less traction among institutions than it deserves. OER has been promoted and supported as an organized movement since 2001, and though it is still relatively "young" (D'Antoni, 2009) but "well established" (Ferguson et al, 2017), its impact has not transformed the higher ed landscape to the level that early advocates had anticipated. Certainly, OER is still a substantial topic, particularly in distance education circles, but as is evident in the massive growth in the digital materials market, publishers have managed to effectively convince faculty that the value of their proprietary media platforms are worth the costs to students.

Among the challenges here is the business model of OER: typically, there isn't one, and when there is, it's simply not a lucrative endeavor, especially when compared to the traditional academic publishing market. While some organizations, such as OpenStax and OER Commons, have managed to persist in this landscape and offer a robust catalog of materials, the long-term game here requires significant work in the form of ongoing updates to keep materials current, and this can understandably give pause to individuals and organizations wishing to contribute their work to OER projects. Further, this is also a very valid reason that faculty may decide *not* to adopt an OER resource or platform for their course; why build an entire curriculum around something that may be outdated in a couple years?

The very reason OER advocates had high hopes ties directly to the focus of this chapter: modern media platforms mean that providing no-cost materials is easier than it has ever been. Even with basic search engines, or tools such as Google Scholar, faculty and students have simple and very direct access to an endless stream of content, including primary sources, journal articles, videos, and more. The ability to customize course materials using OER is an incredible opportunity for the academy.

This, though, is also a critical challenge: compiling OER resources can be an overwhelming venture. Compared to selecting a publisher resource, which is normally already quite complete, "building" one's own package of course materials takes time—and it's not just a one-and-done effort, as content can come and go, links change, and so forth. Further, even with a finished package of OER content, the result is often tied to an institution's learning management system, limiting portability. A publisher's media platform is typically a self-contained product, and though LMS integration is typically possible, faculty who may change institutions can face challenges if all of their course-building work is locked into a given LMS, with no guarantee of cross-system compatibility.

For these reasons and others, OER use is not as widespread as it could be, and its adoption has experienced a kind of stalling out, particularly as it competes against cutting-edge features such as proprietary adaptive learning products, which require huge teams of product developers. Even so, if institutions truly care about doing what is best for students, they would re-examine whether course material costs are justified in the larger context of the digital resource landscape. This is by no means a call to doubt the importance of academic texts or published sources to supplement instruction in higher education; it is simply a reminder that course materials, now more media platforms, represent an immensely expansive landscape in the practice of teaching. The choices faculty have here are more substantial, varied, and accessible than they've ever been in the history of the world. The move from printed textbooks to a more nebulous cloud-based approach to course materials is not an inherently bad thing; just the opposite: the promise of these platforms is extraordinary. Faculty must recognize their central role in this market, and also their capability to be catalysts for a synthesis of the old and the new, in a way that is both academically responsible, and respectful of the pressures on student finances.

Ponder

When was the last time your department had an honest discussion about its textbook choices—costs, ethics, quality, etc.? If it has been a while, what is keeping that conversation from happening?

_____
_____
_____
_____
_____
_____
_____
_____

How serious do you take student feedback about the media utilized in your courses, including textbooks?

_____
_____

What are the primary determinants of the course materials you've chosen? How often is that choice revisited?

Do institutional supports, such as instructional design staff, exist to assist in reviewing, selecting, or even developing course material packages?

How seriously, or recently, have you considered open education resources (OER)?

References

D'Antoni, S. (2009). Open Educational Resources: Reviewing initiatives and issues. *Open Learning: The Journal of Open, Distance and e-Learning, 24*:1, 3-10

Ferguson, R., Barzilai, S., Ben-Zvi, D., Chinn, C.A., Herodotou, C., Hod, Y., Kali, Y., Kukulska-Hulme, A., Kupermintz, H., McAndrew, P., Rienties, B., Sagy, O., Scanlon, E., Sharples, M., Weller, M., & Whitelock, D. (2017). Innovating Pedagogy 2017: Open University Innovation Report 6. Milton Keynes: The Open University, UK.

Teaching and Learning

Teaching at Scale

The economics of higher education have become increasingly complex, and the stakes tremendously dire; institutional existence is no longer a basic guarantee as enrollment declines have trended nationwide. Colleges and universities are facing the call to boost efficiency, which has never been an easy pill to swallow at the postsecondary level. Yet, these days, for every earnest department discussion about intentionally reducing class sizes in a coming semester, it seems there are easily two or three conversations—perhaps even at the same institution—about whether classes will even run next time, due to the need to reduce offerings, shutter programs, or even face institutional closure altogether. The disruptive market forces afflicting traditional colleges and universities continue to tighten their hold, but the results may only become apparent to students when they trigger a larger, more conspicuous reduction in service or program offerings. Students don't keep tabs on the ebb and flow of their institution's FTE, while even relatively small changes in those figures can send shudders of fear through faculty and administration who well understand the consequences.

For those entrusted with the operational health of an institution, those numbers really do matter; when demand dries up, supply must adapt. Among the most direct adjustments to be made to mitigate this natural law of capitalism is to squeeze more revenue out of existing streams, and in the context of teaching, this translates into bigger classes. When a breadth of programs is not sustainable, many institutions have sought to rein in the variety, identify their strengths, and scale up in those areas.

The pursuit of larger scale is a significant business decision, even if the goal is only to ensure the lights stay on for the long-term. Certainly, upscaling operational strong points can make very good business sense. In higher education, though, the resulting burden can fall disproportionately on faculty, whose work is truly where the rubber meets the road when classes become larger but personnel levels remain flat.

Is there a way to effectively scale up an institution's academic delivery in a way that supports operational sustainability, quality teaching, *and* faculty sanity? It depends on whom you ask, but as may be expected, many of the institutions attempting to accomplish this are leveraging new technologies and delivery models, with promising results (again, depending on whom you ask). Still, it's anything but easy. This chapter identifies a number of trends emerging as institutions seek to "scale up" their educational delivery models.

The Severity of Scale

Typically, faculty are not fond of the word "scale," often equating that word with more work and less time to do it. Logically, that can mean a poorer experience for the student, and faculty are to be commended for coming to the table on this topic with some healthy skepticism—for their own well-being, as well as for the academic experience as a whole. At the same time, those in administrative roles can put too much faith in the hope that scaling up operations will create a highly efficient system that can be managed more or less in the same way it always has.

Prior to the development of current technologies commonly utilized to upscale program delivery, this path typically began with faculty teaching either more classes, or larger ones, until the institution hired more faculty. Indeed, this is still a common truth today. Most recently, upscaling an academic program has been accomplished through online courses and programs.

Granted, the last decade has seen no small number of diploma mills and for-profits that capitalized on the ability to leverage online learning to further the institution's breadth without the appropriate amount of depth (read: quality). Fortunately, many of these have since disintegrated due to tighter regulations and natural market forces, and bad apples shouldn't be allowed to ruin the promise of upscaling education. And make no mistake, there's plenty of promise here. When done well, teaching at scale can grow an institution, expand its reach, further its mission in a community, and simply do more of what it does, on a bigger stage. When done poorly, teaching at scale can divide a campus, waste resources, sour a community, confuse an institution's identity, and disrupt its mission. The stakes are immensely high.

Further, when institutions dedicate a large amount of resources to scaling up their operations, and that endeavor does not pan out as hoped, the trauma from the failure can paralyze; even the fear of failure can cause a similar state. However, more and more higher education stakeholders are finding that risk aversion is not a viable option. Indeed, risk aversion is itself more of a risk in this field than it ever has been before. Of all the options that may be on the table, utilizing new models and technologies to operate on a larger scale may be the option with the lowest entry barrier. Rather than experimenting with new high-demand programs, an institution can double-down on what it already have in place.

Perhaps because of this, the business of teaching at scale is booming. In the distance education world, Online Program Managers (OPMs) seek to provide institutions with solutions to the logistics of scaling up: marketing, recruitment, course development, seed funding, etc. While the topic of third-party partners is a timely one, this chapter focuses more intently on the variables of teaching and learning when institutions consider scaling up what they do.

Multimedia

Though sometimes begrudgingly, faculty have continued to embrace the reinvention of the traditional lecture, in the form of content delivery that is more dynamic and perhaps more beneficial to student learning. Lately, these kinds of efforts often hinge on digital materials, regardless of the course's primary modality. The same tools that make this possible also ease challenges to the instructor, with important implications for increasing the scale of teaching.

The evolution of digital media, including high-definition images and video, high-precision maps, high-fidelity audio recordings, and the ability to connect with thousands of other visitors via social media, means that learners can tap into an incredible amount of information about any topic, from a distance. Further, once compiled, all of this media can be collected, replicated, shared, and "consumed" by countless others, with the push of a button. Someone who wants to learn about Scotland can know everything there is to know, with the exception of the feeling of its ground under their feet, before they ever set foot on its soil. We truly live in amazing times.

When higher education is considered with this in mind, the picture should be more promising than it often is perceived to be. In the same way as one would learn about the Highlands, faculty can fashion a digital experience as never before, to supplement their teaching, or, yes, even replace it entirely. An effective multimedia portfolio can paint an impressive picture of whatever subject is being taught. For many courses, particularly of the introductory or survey type, this digital portfolio can largely replace traditional lectures, and it has. Further—and this is the big kicker—digital materials can be collected and reviewed and shared ad infinitum.

This concept often grates against the collective faculty consciousness. If faculty are producers of finite content rather than regular concierges of knowledge (at least on a semester basis), is not their very profession at risk? Is the art of "professing" obsolete? Does education devolve into YouTube? By replacing their lectures with recordings and more exciting forms of media, are faculty digging their own grave?

The answer is, "It depends." In many cases, yes, and in many cases, no. Have face-to-face guitar lessons disappeared from the face of the Earth, now that YouTube boasts millions of introductory guitar videos? Rather, guitar teachers have gained a powerful new platform to utilize in sharing their knowledge. If anything, the future is bright for individuals who love to teach, and are willing and capable to utilize modern tools to tell stories about subjects they love. The teaching profession will evolve—it always has, albeit slowly—and educators should be thrilled that technology allows their work, or even just information about the topics they love, to be communicated and shared so easily, in so many dynamic and engaging ways.

Teaching at scale is about doing just that: leveraging available tools and platforms to bring more learners to the feasting table, even if someone else made the food. Truth be told, attempting to increase the scale of a program through traditional delivery methods—traditional lectures, more classes, and more faculty—is far less sustainable of a model than it used to be. Digital media can play a key role in this expansion that allows faculty to spend their time in other ways as they guide more students through the learning process. At the same time, it's not the only option faculty have to upscale program delivery.

Web-Conferencing

Technically, provided the audience is there, a traditional class can be scaled up in an afternoon with only an Internet connection and some web space, as colleges have been doing for decades now with their learning management systems (LMS). What continues to drastically improve is the ability to translate a face-to-face experience to a digital audience, to provide an experience that is very similar to what one would expect in a traditional classroom.

This gap has been filled by the web-conferencing tool, undoubtedly one of the most important developments in teaching at scale, providing an expansive dimension of interactivity in a relatively efficient way. In truth, web-conferencing tools themselves are no longer perceived as an innovation; now that these platforms have reached a point of near perfection, the benefits they provide to faculty—particularly in distance modalities—mean that no self-respecting institution can be without one. Such platforms allow a channel for faculty to conduct classes from a distance in even greater fidelity, leveraging audio/video streams to provide a kind of presence and interpersonal experience that was often lacking when online classes centered on only the LMS. Modern products such as Skype for Business, Zoom, GoToMeeting, and Adobe Connect are only a handful of the dozens, if not hundreds, of tools now used routinely by colleges and universities to deliver education on a larger scale, electronically.

Many institutions have invested in scaled delivery models intentionally centered on web-conferencing platforms, allowing students to develop small groups and cohorts within a significantly larger class size. These are often accomplished through virtual breakout sessions, as utilized in Stanford University's continuing studies programs, or the University of Tennessee's online executive MBA, social work, and nursing programs (Hart, 2015). Even if students in those groups never physically meet, those connections matter, and can create community where there otherwise would be none, as has often been the case in asynchronous classes that relied only on the institution's LMS. No longer are students just a name on a roster, or the author of a forum post. Moving faces and synchronous conversation—even through a somewhat-pixelated video feed—provides an experience that is leaps and bounds beyond online classes of the past, and can even prove more engaging than a cavernous lecture hall.

The breakout session functionality of web-conferencing solutions can effectively shrink a large class into a much smaller one, by limiting the number of students present in a session at a given time. Whereas dozens may be officially enrolled in the class, the utilization of virtual small groups ensures that those student only see their classmates within their designated groups. The instructor can provide all materials through digital media, assign activities to the small groups, and then either join the individual groups to engage in a virtual flipped classroom, or invite the students to a plenary session where all groups can be addressed collectively. By customizing the web-conferencing settings, students may never know just how large the class actually is, and if the instructor is strategic in utilizing and delivering the other aspects of the course, students may enjoy all the benefits of a smaller class, despite the actual length of the roster.

Adaptive Learning

A final trend related to teaching at scale is the rise of adaptive learning, birthed through the marriage of digital course materials and artificial intelligence. This is among the most exciting of developments in scalable teaching, as well as one of the most terrifying. As touched upon in a previous chapter, adaptive learning describes the ability of digital course materials to adjust themselves in response to student feedback. Imagine a course text with supplemental activities meant to gauge the student's understanding. If a student is able to establish through predetermined criteria that they've learned what they're supposed to learn, and the unit outcomes have been demonstrated, the materials "know" that the student's pathway should be either abbreviated or extended, and adjusts accordingly, without the actual instructor having to do anything beyond setting up those initial thresholds.

Adaptive learning carries with it the possibility to revolutionize teaching at scale. In the past, faculty may have struggled to assess how well students were "getting" the material. In distance education, this became infinitely more complicated; teachers couldn't simply wander around a room during a course activity and look over students' shoulders. With adaptive course technologies, faculty can allow the course materials to take on a life of their own and assess student understanding, in more targeted and accurate formative methods, rather than through traditional summative assessments. Particularly at lower-level and survey courses, adaptive course materials can significantly lighten the load for the faculty, freeing that person to engage students in other ways, providing more timely, directed, and efficient kinds of intervention.

Caution

The trends identified in this chapter represent an exciting array of developments in teaching at scale, and as more institutions take action to ensure long-term viability, these will continue to be adapted, and new approaches will emerge. As decision-makers consider how they will meet the demands of teaching at larger scale, two variables should be attended with great care: the individual learner, and institutional identity.

A conversation about teaching at scale would be remiss without considering the learner. As has been mentioned, one of the most commonly-cited faculty concerns about scaling up an institution's delivery models is the detrimental effect this can have on students. While extending the opportunity to more learners may be important to both the institution as well as the actual students who pursue that opportunity, students don't want to be lost in a crowd. If institutions take action to increase their enrollment, they cannot neglect the appropriate measures to not only support those added students academically, but to also affirm their place in the campus community, regardless of how the course is delivered.

Finally, scaling up can have direct implications not just on program size, but also institutional identity. Many colleges and universities have spent the past two decades struggling with the transition from a completely tangible institution to one that exists partly online, and for institutions that begin to take deeper steps in that direction, aspects that are central to the community's DNA can begin to be neglected. For this reason, when the decision is made to scale up in program delivery, whatever it is that makes the institution unique must be carefully baked into whatever strategies are employed to expand in scale.

Ponder

Is your institution considering increasing the scale of its operations? What is driving the institution toward or away from this interest?

_____
_____
_____
_____
_____

How big is too big? What would be considered a successful class and/or institution size?

How would your institution be perceived differently if it were to increase in size and scale?

At what point does size hinder mission? Under what conditions?

How risky is this endeavor? Will the institution be OK if the endeavor fails?

_____
_____
_____
_____
_____
_____

Who are the loudest detractors of a larger scale, and what are their concerns?

_____
_____
_____
_____
_____
_____

What is the weakest link in an up-scaled infrastructure, and how will it be addressed?

_____
_____
_____
_____
_____
_____

References

Hart, M. (2015). *New technology allows breakout sessions for large online video classes.* Campus Technology. Retrieved from https://campustechnology.com/articles/2015/12/01/new-technology-allows-breakout-sessions-for-large-online-video-classes.aspx.

Teaching and Learning

Pedagogical Strategies I: Deconstructing the Traditional

The final two chapters of this section highlight a selection of trending pedagogical strategies. This chapter analyzes two such trends, with a common thread being the deconstruction of long-standing norms in post-secondary education, namely the structures surrounding instruction. Here, we will briefly examine competency-based education and open learning.

Competency-Based Education

Throughout the second decade of the twenty-first century, postsecondary institutions have increasingly sought to attract populations more diverse than the traditional undergraduate student who lives on campus, studies full-time, and graduates in four years. For many, this has been a necessity, in response to increased competition and a dwindling pool of the kinds of students that have long filled college classrooms. As growth in that population has started to level off, sights have been set on nontraditional populations, such as working adults and transfer students.

These populations often bring with them a wealth of life experience and skill sets that may overlap with learning goals embedded in the programs in which they enroll. For those students, the ideal institution would offer a program willing to recognize and validate that pre-existing knowledge, and allow the opportunity to shorten their time to program completion. It's a starkly rational idea; how should that work?

Granted, most institutions do have some kind of basic mechanism to allow students to earn credit for what they already know, though these are limited, commonly found in challenge assessments or other "testing out" options. Further, many of these are directed specifically at traditional students, such as through Advanced Placement (AP) exams in high school. However, over the last several years, competency-based education (CBE) has gained a significant amount of traction as a pedagogical strategy in mainstream higher education, providing a win-win-win solution for students, employers, and institutions, and providing an option that is more fitting and appropriate to nontraditional students.

Competency-based education builds assessment of previously-acquired knowledge and skills into courses themselves, tying learning outcomes to skill-based competencies; if a student has obtained knowledge, either in the classroom or elsewhere, that student is given the opportunity within an individual course context to demonstrate that knowledge by satisfying certain conditions set by the instructor. They can then move on to the next learning goal, potentially skipping a large amount of the curriculum. Thus, if the student comes into the course with various experiences and knowledge, the student would be able to demonstrate what they know, but still learn what they don't. CBE requires that instruction be laser-focused on learning objectives, which is also proving to have important implications for the length of academic programs.

Long a common method of assessment in trade schools and skills-based programs at two-year colleges, CBE has found its latest groove in online education, particularly because of that modality's ability to better manage multiple varying pathways, compared with a face-to-face program. Digital platforms now allow a single course and its materials to be highly personalized and adaptable—far beyond what would be possible in a traditional classroom full of students.

CBE is a pedagogical strategy more than it is a delivery model, and it has significant implications for faculty. "Because CBE often departs from traditional models of teaching and learning, CBE programs frequently involve restructuring typical faculty roles" (Lurie, Mason, & Parsons, 2018, p.13). Certainly, an instructor can no longer rely on a simple chronological lesson plan, divided over a traditional fifteen- or sixteen-week semester; students could potentially finish the entire course in half the time, or even less. Ideally, a CBE class must be traversable at greater speed (hence the trend toward digital delivery), lest students spend much of the semester waiting around after demonstrating competency long before their classmates.

The faculty role in a CBE course may involve a number of tasks beyond traditional teaching, ranging from a greater focus on assessment and evaluating competencies, to coaching or mentoring students as they navigate a less linear pathway. When teaching a CBE-enabled course, faculty must be prepared for students to be at various states of learning and completion, and the amount of communication may vary tremendously from student to student. If a student demonstrates that a given learning outcome has already been met through prior learning, essentially, there may be no real reason for the student and instructor to interact on that particular sub-topic. This carries with it the common concerns about online learning in general, though: what aspects of traditional classroom learning are lost? Certainly, if students are all proceeding at various paces, the opportunities for them to interact may be few and far between. Providing optional venues for interaction and peer engagement are easily accomplished in online delivery, but when students have the opportunity to zip through at their own pace, and have sought a modality that allows them to do that, the odds of collaboration are diminished. Indeed, faculty have often encountered this difficulty when implementing CBE as a pedagogy.

The question naturally arises, how critical is interpersonal engagement in higher education, both in a pedagogical faculty-student sense, as well as a learner-learner sense? While some institutions have found success in integrating CBE into face-to-face programs—long "business as usual" at the nation's technical schools—others, especially traditional colleges and universities, may balk at a delivery mode that stands to isolate its students as they learn, which runs counter-culturally to the zeitgeist of more social educational experiences. For those seeking to deliver an academic experience that supports or contributes to a campus culture or identity, CBE can be a true conundrum.

Power brokers in the online learning world, including Western Governors University and Southern New Hampshire University, have long dominated in this arena, and have gotten quite good at it, as evident in their completion and satisfaction rates. Those institutions may rely on dedicated student coaches to supplement the interpersonal contact that may be lacking in individual classes. Other more traditional institutions have waded into CBE initiatives, though the going has often been slow and laborious for a variety of reasons, including federal restrictions on financial aid. However, such restrictions have only relaxed with time, and more and more institutions are establishing successful CBE programs, often reaching populations previously underserved by the school.

While decisions to structure an academic program as competency-based must typically be made at the program level, in order to ensure consistency across classes, the success or failure of this pedagogy lies in the way in which the curriculum is laid out, and the pathways students are able to navigate. This can be a complex technical endeavor, which is one of the reasons faculty have increasingly looked to publishers for help. Unsurprisingly, CBE has been a driving market of adaptive learning solutions.

One of the leading organizations behind CBE adoption is the Competency-Based Education Network, or C-BEN. Among its roles is service as a data clearinghouse for CBE initiatives; it recently published its findings of the 2018 National Survey of Postsecondary Competency-Based Education, to illustrate the current state of the field. In the document summarizing the results of that survey—essential reading for those who may be further interested in CBE—the authors note the difficulty in identifying every CBE program in the nation, relying on survey respondents to help paint a clearer picture of the scope of CBE and trends surrounding this topic. Of the 501 respondent institutions of that survey, only fifty-seven reported currently operating at least one full CBE program, though across those institutions, 512 CBE programs were in operations, revealing the high concentration of programs at a small number of schools. 430 institutions (including those that were already operating such programs) reported interest in CBE, while 71 expressed no interest. These are not staggering numbers, but they do represent a notable slice of the higher education sector.

As institutions grapple with ways to better articulate the value of a postsecondary degree, CBE is poised to offer appealing benefits, both for the experienced student who wishes to shorten their time to a degree, as well as the faculty who seek to validate what those students already know, even if that means sending them through to the next stage in their studies. Because CBE is a pedagogy that can be implemented in individual classes, faculty do not have to wait for their department to agree on this method as a program-wide mechanism of delivery. Despite this ability to adopt CBE at the course level, the pedagogy still faces significant barriers in adoption and acceleration. However, its "learner-centric logic…remains compelling for many institutions," as well as for many faculty (Lurie, Mason, & Parsons, 2018).

Open Learning

If competency-based education turns higher education on its head by shortcutting traditional curricular pathways, pedagogies centered on concepts of open learning can spin the field even further, effectively rolling it down the hill. The term "open learning," or "open educational practices," naturally lacks the specificity of other theoretical pedagogies, and blurs the line between delivery model and pedagogy. This concept represents the deconstruction of traditional educational structures—tangible or not—in formal learning processes. Having first emerged conceptually in the 1970s, open learning can refer to a number of different pedagogies and related variables, including procedural, instructional, or supplemental to educational experiences. This rapidly-increasing category includes an extensive list of possibilities, including the following, to name a few: loosely structured curricular pathways in which students determine on their own what to study and how to proceed; courses without set end dates; courses that utilize open education resources (OER) as a major component; and low- or no-barrier entry requirements for academic programs.

Those approaches have yielded programs and concepts that are becoming increasingly familiar to higher education practitioners, such as customized "build-your-own-degree" pathways, massively open online courses (MOOCs), and test-optional admissions policies. Granted, many such endeavors are still in their formative stages, but not every concept of open learning has proved to have staying power. MOOCs were all the rage around 2012, with so-called "futurists" rushing to hail them as the end of higher education as we knew it, only to see the entire movement putter out and primarily transform into a recruitment strategy for large institutions, with some notable exceptions. For the other 90% of higher education institutions, life went on.

Even so, the rise-and-fall of MOOCs illustrates a challenge of open educational practices: the postsecondary world is very used to parameters, and when things go off the rails, we're not quite sure what to expect, or how to respond. Further, accreditors have been notoriously hesitant to allow colleges to stray too far from traditional norms and structures, without an abundance of proof of preparedness. For example, if an institution decides to go test-optional, as more and more institutions are choosing to do, the proper academic student supports must be in place to properly serve students who may then qualify for admission. Otherwise, the institution will have a difficult time making the case to their accreditor that their obligation to those students was met. Yet, when institutions step outside of their box, they encounter all sorts of novel challenges, even in well-trod topics such as academic support.

Organizations focused on open learning, such as the United Kingdom's Open University, which recently celebrated its fiftieth anniversary, have provided important research and support to institutional endeavors to deliver education in more open ways, since those methods often require a level of risk to which many institutions are unaccustomed. Many such organizations are tied to more specific versions of open learning, such as the Competency-Based Education Network or the Open Education Resource (OER) Foundation.

Additionally, open learning as a pedagogy can prove immensely challenging for faculty, as the ability to oversee student learning is either naturally or intentionally more limited. Here, faculty are less sources of knowledge, and more guides—sometimes little-used—as students learn about topics of their own choosing or develop their own learning goals as well as their own pathways to reach them. Open learning practices have been part of the landscape for a long time, though in a very narrow or restricted sense, as in allowing students to choose essay topics or enroll in directed study courses. This pedagogy is becoming substantially more enabled through greater flexibility in communication technologies, which allow students to be less tethered to a place, without restricting their ability to consume information or connect interpersonally as needed. As these trends continue, increasingly, students will be better equipped to determine and pursue their own studies more openly and independently, outside the confines of traditional academic pathways and procedures. Institutions that acknowledge and prepare for this reality will be poised to have a role in its future.

Ponder

The term "competencies" can be a loaded one for faculty, as it has historically been tied to technical and trade education, rather than the liberal arts. Yet, competency-based education can be just as applicable to liberal arts programs. What is your institution's pulse on competency-based education? Has this discussion gained any traction, or even begun?

_____
_____
_____
_____
_____
_____
_____
_____

Should students in a given program be forced to take a "required" course, even if they already possess the knowledge or skills it teaches? Does your institution have mechanisms in place to encourage students to reflect on whether or not they have already obtained that knowledge, or does the institution systemically usher students through similar experiences? Is there an ethical concern to this?

_____
_____
_____
_____
_____
_____
_____
_____

Why is open learning unsettling to many in academia? Are its benefits worth an intentional campus discussion?

_____
_____
_____
_____

Consider taking an inventory of open learning practices on campus, and sharing those with your department or sphere of influence.

References

Cronin, C. (2017). Openness and praxis: Exploring the use of open educational practices in higher education. *The International Review of Research in Open and Distributed Learning, 18*(5). DOI: 10.19173/irrodl.v18i5.3096

Ferguson, R., Barzilai, S., Ben-Zvi, D., Chinn, C.A., Herodotou, C., Hod, Y., Kali, Y., Kukulska-Hulme, A., Kupermintz, H., McAndrew, P., Rienties, B., Sagy, O., Scanlon, E., Sharples, M., Weller, M., & Whitelock, D. (2017). *Innovating Pedagogy 2017: Open University Innovation Report 6.* Milton Keynes: The Open University, UK.

Ferguson, R., Coughlan, T., Egelandsdal, K., Gaved, M., Herodotou, C., Hillaire, G., Jones, D., Jowers, I., Kukulska-Hulme, A., McAndrew, P., Misiejuk, K., Ness, I. J., Rienties, B., Scanlon, E., Sharples, M., Wasson, B., Weller, M. and Whitelock, D. (2019). *Innovating Pedagogy 2019: Open University Innovation Report 7.* Milton Keynes: The Open University, UK.

Lurie, H., Mason, J., and Parsons, K. (2018). *Findings from the 2018 National Survey of Postsecondary Competency-Based Education.* American Institutes for Research & Encoura Eduventures Research. Retrieved from https://cberesearch.org/sites/default/files/2019-01/National%20Survey%20of%20Postsec%20CBE%20-%20 2018%20-%20AIR-Eduventures%20-%20Final.pdf

Teaching and Learning

Pedagogical Strategies II: Gamification & Immersive Learning

Innovation in postsecondary teaching and learning does not have to rely on chipping away at traditional structures and practices, many of which have withstood the test of time and continue to prove valuable and effective. As the twenty-first century has unfurled and higher education stakeholders look at time-honored practices with fresh eyes and new perspectives amidst a rapidly shifting landscape, many have sought to approach teaching in new ways, or to introduce new variables into seemingly tired equations, constructing new norms that are a synthesis of past and present. As has been a recurring theme in this section, current technologies allow educators a level of creativity never before possible. This chapter examines two creatively constructive pedagogies that have emerged amidst this backdrop of possibilities: gamification, and immersive learning.

Gamification

In an era in which students are more tied to devices than they are their closest friends, gaming has received a massive boost from the prevalence of mobile devices and both the ease of access and relatively low entry cost of mobile gaming. The demographics of "gamers" has shifted significantly, too. Whereas electronic games largely targeted male youth and teens in the last couple decades of the twentieth century, the gaming audience counts among its members a broad swath of the global population, numbering over 2 billion people. According to one study, surprisingly, only 37% of mobile gamers are men; over half are in their fifties, with only 8% being teenagers. Further, as of 2019, approximately 74% of Apple's iTunes revenues came from mobile games (Dobrilova, 2019).

These statistics do not account for the traditional console video gaming sector of the industry, which may still somewhat resemble the demographics of ten or twenty years ago, but the statistics of the mobile gaming industry illustrate just how common electronic games have become in the twenty-first century, at least in the context of the smartphone revolution. An incredible number of people play games on their devices, likely spending far more time engrossed in games than using the device to speak to another human being—its original intended use.

While mobile gaming is a recent global phenomenon, the concept of "gamifying" education has existed for a long time—it may even be prehistoric, as children have long learned from play. At the same time that games began to incorporate a wider variety of multimedia that was also more interactive, the higher education landscape began its shift to digital delivery, and, naturally, it was only a matter of time before the two converged in some fashion.

Many elements of gaming have found their way into higher education, separately, over time: objectives, points, and teams are all routine concepts in this landscape. More recently, reward systems have shifted to focus less on competition, and more on individual achievement, exemplified in the rise of the badge. Perhaps most crucially, the Internet and the ubiquity of handheld devices have provided a platform that is nearly universal and filled with creativity, shareable content, and capitalism-driven solutions for education that speak directly to the ballooning market of educators seeking to more effectively engage their students through technology-based activities and games. No longer must those individuals rely on their own ideas or resourcefulness; a simple app search provides nearly endless solutions.

As a pedagogical strategy, educators engage students in a wide variety of games or game-like activities. An early iteration of this involved students purchasing "clicker" hand-held devices that allowed them to respond to prompts in-class, often in a lecture or survey format, with the results aggregated and visualized immediately on a projected screen. These specialized devices have since been firmly supplanted by smartphones, allowing students to participate in these kinds of responsive activities, often competitively with the rest of their classmates, at a moment's notice, particularly if the instructor feels like the class' attention is waning. One of the larger and more successful of these third-party app-based student response platforms is called Kahoot, which fully embraces its game-based roots.

As in that example, many faculty utilize games in class in supplemental or minor ways. Rarer, but far more intriguing, are cases in which faculty structure the entire class as a kind of game, in which students accumulate scores rather than grades, perhaps with a kind of class-wide leaderboard identifying the top-scoring students. Lessons may be delivered as role-playing scenarios, with the instructor occupying a role akin to a dungeon master in Dungeons and Dragons. These wholesale overhauls of the class experience can be complex, time-consuming, and even exhausting, but students are likely to remember the experience, and, by extension, the learning objectives the game teaches.

Some of the biggest names in educational games on digital platforms aren't necessarily specific to the higher education scene, but occupy a large role, and have greatly influenced subsequent products that have since been developed. These include the vast interdisciplinary catalog of Khan Academy and the language learning app platform Duolingo. Traditional academic publishers have jumped into this arena as well. As discussed in a previous chapter, as digital course materials have evolved, interactivity has proved king, and this trend has shifted to a more game-oriented approach when delivering content. Digital course materials now regularly incorporate progress bars and skill maps, similar to mechanics found in all manner of games that play to participants' desire to unlock subsequent levels of difficulty, collect digital rewards, and reach visualized ends. Many of these have long been present in Khan Academy, and its meteoric and persistent success provides further evidence of the value of entertaining education.

No signs suggest the role of games in education will decrease in the future, and in fact, it seems the opposite is likely, particularly in light of the next, and final, topic in this section: immersive learning.

Immersive Learning

Truly immersive learning has long straddled the fence between reality and science fiction. When video gaming rose to prominence through the 1980s and 1990s, tech-focused educators saw the promise in a level of computer-generated realism that would allow game developers to essentially create immersive new worlds, once the fidelity of digital gaming reached a sufficient level. Over the last four decades, we have slowly but surely inched in the direction of that future, though it has proved to be a longer road than many anticipated. Today, virtual reality (VR), augmented reality (AR), and simulation technologies seem absolutely poised to take higher education to a level beyond the wildest dreams of the last hundred years.

It almost didn't happen, though. In the mid-1990s, virtual reality experienced a false start across the industry. The idea of virtual reality had gained traction widely and rapidly, but unfortunately, the technology was simply unprepared for the plans eager VR advocates had formulated—not just for education, but for entertainment purposes, too. Huge, clunky VR setups with poor, pixelated resolutions dotted shopping malls and tourist locations, charging steep sums for short experiences that were somewhat novel, but nothing transformative. VR in the 1990s was little more than a fad, eventually disintegrating altogether.

Today, it's a far different story. Technology is faster, stronger, smaller, and more portable and less tethered than it has ever been, providing a kind of perfect storm for virtual reality and augmented reality to truly take hold by accomplishing intended goals truly effectively, and in high definition. In the gaming industry, virtual reality sets are already available and affordable on the consumer market, in the form of products such as the Oculus Rift and HTC Vive. With these, gamers can enjoy a level of immersion far beyond what they've been able to enjoy so far, sitting on a couch in front of a large-screen TV.

The implications of VR/AR for entertainment are self-evident, as they may be for education, too. However, high-quality VR/AR experiences for any medium require a heavy investment of time and funding for software development. These kinds of experiences don't create themselves, and require capabilities far beyond the average educator. Thus, the VR/AR industry is currently in somewhat of a holding pattern as developers engage in their craft. Because of the rapidness at which the device landscape changes, this will be the site of an immense degree of change in the next few years, as those developers struggle to develop for the most current or bleeding-edge hardware specifications—a moving target. As such, educators may benefit from a healthy dose of caution, resisting the urge to purchase current VR/AR hardware until the most widely-supported products become more evident.

Because the resurgence of virtual reality, and the rise of augmented reality, have taken place in a post-social-networking society, VR/AR also hold great promise for providing high-fidelity experiences that are also capable of connecting learners across distances, fusing together some of the best aspects and benefits of online learning with social media. According to Ferguson et al (2017):

> *In VR, learners can become avatars interacting with other avatars. They can travel through time and space. They can play 'what if?', by exploring possibilities that cannot be set up in real life. They can engage in activities that would be difficult, dangerous or impossible in everyday life. Game elements are often involved. (p.26)*

A third platform of immersive pedagogy receives far less media coverage, but has already proven its worth in the classroom: simulation. Such products are already widely used at higher education institutions, and many such practices have historically relied little on technology, at least of the digital kind. In nursing programs across the United States, it's not uncommon to see what many would assume is a simple mannequin, but which simulation professionals would recognize as an effective (and expensive) piece of high-fidelity simulation equipment. Simulation in healthcare education is widely accepted as an innovative and effective approach to teaching, particularly in nursing (Kim, Park, & Shin, 2016).

The rise and success of mechanical simulation in pedagogy has set the stage for its next iteration, made possible through advances in virtual and augmented reality: digital and VR/AR simulation. Currently, start-ups and well-established corporations alike are engaged in a kind of arms race to become a leader in digital simulation for various education and training industries, not least of which includes healthcare, and particularly nursing and other medical disciplines.

Undoubtedly, immersive learning is one of the most exciting topics in all of higher education, and warrants a level of attention that many wish they'd devoted to online education in its formative years. For postsecondary futurists who have often wondered what the next big thing will be in teaching and learning at colleges and universities—whatever they may look like over the next many years—immersive learning is a trend to follow.

Ponder

Gamification as a pedagogy can naturally be an enjoyable endeavor for all involved, both students as well as faculty. Why might your colleagues frown on this method of teaching, or at least undervalue it?

_____
_____
_____

What resources exist on your campus to investigate possibilities to utilize games in course contexts?

Faculty may be hesitant to utilize third-party products, even well-known apps, in the classroom, due to a variety of reasons, including costs, device equity, accessibility, etc. These are important discussions to be having; consider convening faculty to talk about these issues and identify best practices for the institution.

With the reinvigoration of virtual/augmented reality in recent years, education may look very different in ten years, quite literally. Has your institution begun to consider opportunities in this area? Why or why not?

_____
_____
_____
_____
_____
_____
_____

What kinds of skills will VR/AR require for faculty in the future? Has your institution begun to support or provide appropriate professional development opportunities?

_____
_____
_____
_____
_____
_____
_____

References

Bruenner, E. (2011). *Play to learn with Khan Academy.* Gamification Co. Retrieved from http://www.gamification.co/2011/05/26/quests-skill-trees-for-learning-with-khan-academy/.

Dobrilova, T. (2019). *14 Mobile gaming statistics, 2019 – Insights into $2.2B gamers market.* Techjury.Net. Retrieved from https://techjury.net/stats-about/mobile-gaming/.

Ferguson, R., Barzilai, S., Ben-Zvi, D., Chinn, C.A., Herodotou, C., Hod, Y., Kali, Y., Kukulska-Hulme, A., Kupermintz, H., McAndrew, P., Rienties, B., Sagy, O., Scanlon, E., Sharples, M., Weller, M., & Whitelock, D. (2017). *Innovating Pedagogy 2017: Open University Innovation Report 6.* Milton Keynes: The Open University, UK.

Kim, J., Park, J. H., & Shin, S. (2016). Effectiveness of simulation-based nursing education depending on fidelity: A meta-analysis. *BMC Medical Education, 16*, 152. doi:10.1186/s12909-016-0672-7

Sherlock, M. (2017). *Is it all in the game? Gamification in higher education.* ExLibris. Retrieved from https://www.exlibrisgroup.com/game-gamification-higher-education-mobile/

About the Authors

Michael G. Strawser, Ph.D., currently serves as an Assistant Professor of Communication and the Deputy Assistant Director overseeing Curriculum and Instruction in the Nicholson School of Communication and Media at the University of Central Florida. Before his time at UCF, Dr. Strawser was the Director of Graduate Programs and an Assistant Professor of Communication at Bellarmine University in Louisville, KY. Dr. Strawser's previous books include *Engaging Millennial Faculty* (New Forums Press) and edited volumes: *New Media and Digital Pedagogy: Enhancing the Twenty-First Century Classroom, Transformative Student Experiences in Higher Education: Meeting the Needs of the Twenty-First Century Student and Modern Workplace*, and *Leading Millennial Faculty: Navigating the New Professoriate* (all with Lexington Books). His research interests broadly include instructional and organizational communication and higher education, specifically faculty development and teaching and learning. Dr. Strawser is also the owner and lead consultant for Legacy Communication Training and Consulting, L.L.C. (www.legacyctc.com).

James D. Breslin, Ph.D., is a higher education scholar, practitioner, and consultant who specializes in student success, academic support and advising, assessment, institutional effectiveness, and leadership and administration. He currently serves as the Assistant Provost for Assessment, Accreditation, and Institutional Effectiveness at Bellarmine University. Dr. Breslin has presented more than 60 conference sessions and published several peer-reviewed articles and book chapters on a variety of topics. Dr. Breslin participates as an active citizen in the field of higher education and has consulted with more than two dozen institutions across the US and beyond. He has served on editorial boards for several peer-reviewed publications and in elected leadership roles in professional organizations. Dr. Breslin has been recognized for his contributions to the field of higher education with multiple awards from associations and funding agencies, and most recently was named a Diamond Honoree by the American College Personnel Association.

Adam Elias currently serves as Director of Innovative Learning Systems at Bellarmine University, a role in which he promotes and supports academic innovation, particularly in the development of the university's distance education initiatives. Adam has spent over ten years in administrative roles in distance education, at both public and private institutions. He is currently pursuing a Ph.D. in Higher Education from the University of Kentucky; his research interests include distance education perceptions and policy, as well as managing change in institutional identity and operations resulting from shifts in instructional models. He has presented at numerous state and national conferences, on topics such as instructional technology, delivery models, and postsecondary trends. His work has been published in *The Chronicle of Higher Education*. The best thing about Adam is the company he keeps: He married his high school sweetheart, Natalie, and they live happily ever after with their two beautiful daughters, in Louisville, Kentucky.

www.ingramcontent.com/pod-product-compliance
Lightning Source LLC
Chambersburg PA
CBHW052341230426
43664CB00041B/2596